INSIDE THE

Mysteries

OF THE

BIBLE

New Perspectives on Ancient Truths

Time Inc. Home Entertainment

Publisher
Richard Fraiman

Executive Director, Marketing Services
Carol Pittard

Director, Retail & Special Sales
Tom Mifsud

Marketing Director, Branded Businesses
Swati Rao

Director, New Product Development
Peter Harper

Financial Director
Steven Sandonato

Assistant General Counsel
Dasha Smith Dwin

Prepress Manager
Emily Rabin

Book Production Manager
Jonathan Polsky

Associate Prepress Manager
Anne-Michelle Gallero

Associate Marketing Manager
Alexandra Bliss

General Editor
Christopher D. Hudson

Senior Editor
Kelly Knauer

Managing Editor
Carol Smith

Consulting Editors from the American Bible Society's Nida Institute for Biblical Study
Barbara Bernstengel
Charles Houser
With special thanks to the American Bible Society's Committee on Translation and Scholarship

Contributing Writers
Stan Campbell
Stephen Clark
Robin Schmidt
Anita Palmer
Kimn Swenson-Golnick
Mia Littlejohn
Shannon Woodward
Carol Smith
Randy Southern

Design and Production
Mark Wainwright
Symbology Creative

special thanks:
Bozena Bannett
Glenn Buonocore
Suzanne Janso
Robert Marasco
Brooke McGuire
Ilene Schreider
Adriana Tierno
Britney Williams

© 2006
Time Inc. Home Entertainment
Time Inc.
1271 Avenue of the Americas
New York, New York 10020

Unless otherwise noted, all Scripture quotations are from the *Holy Bible, Contemporary English Version* (CEV). Copyright 1995 by the American Bible Society. Used by permission of the American Bible Society. All rights reserved.

Scripture quotations marked NIV are taken from the *Holy Bible, New International Version*, copyright © 1973, 1978, 1984 by the International Bible Society. Used by permission of Zondervan. All rights reserved.

ISBN 13: 978-1-933405-91-9
ISBN 10: 1-933405-91-0

We welcome your comments and suggestions about *Inside the Mysteries of the Bible*. Please write to us at:

Inside the Mysteries of the Bible
Attention: Book Editors
PO Box 11016
Des Moines, IA 50336-1016

If you would like to order any of our hardcover Collector's Edition books, please call us at 1-800-327-6388. (Monday through Friday, 7:00 a.m.— 8:00 p.m. or Saturday, 7:00 a.m.— 6:00 p.m. Central Time).

INSIDE THE
Mysteries
OF THE
BIBLE

NEW PERSPECTIVES ON ANCIENT TRUTHS

AMERICAN BIBLE SOCIETY

Time Inc.
HOME ENTERTAINMENT

table of
Contents

introduction

The ancient text we call the Bible is filled with marvels and mysteries, with disasters, cataclysms, and calamities. Yet though the Bible is thousands of years old, the people we meet in its pages are surprisingly similar to us. They struggled. They succeeded. Sometimes they failed. They gloried

in their shining moments and grieved in their dark ones. And, like us, they experienced the unexplained—and sought to understand this world and their place within it.

The Bible tells the story of God, who created a world of natural order, yet didn't always abide by that order. He parted the waters of the sea. He stopped the sun in the sky. He allowed his creations to face the consequences of their actions, and in some cases, he rescued them in the nick of time. At times, he even reversed life's most final process: death.

The words that fill the following pages were written by people who believe in the mysteries they depict. They believe in God and in his interaction with the world he created. They believe that there is a supernatural world as surely as there is a natural one. Yet they've explored the unusual events depicted in the Bible from many angles, including science, history, and faith.

The purpose of these pages is not to explain away the Bible's mysteries, for they were designed to invite conjecture. Instead, the purpose is to examine them from several sides and wonder together what we might learn from them.

After thousands of years, the mysteries of the Bible still have the power to fascinate us, to puzzle us, to delight us. And most important, they remind us that there are surprises to be found in our own lives and our own world, if one has the eyes of faith to see them.

Which Bible?

There are many different versions of the Bible, which has been translated into hundreds of languages. Most versions are identified by an abbreviation. This book is based on a modern English version called the *Contemporary English Version* (CEV), and almost all its citations are drawn from that source. Any citations based on different versions are clearly marked with the most common abbreviation for that version.

> "The most beautiful thing one can experience is the Mysterious. It is truly the basis of all Arts and Sciences."
>
> Albert Einstein

Sources

At the end of this work, you will find a list of sources that were used for research. New historical discoveries continue to enlighten us about the places and people that the Bible describes. Through archaeology, scientific research, and manuscript recovery, we continue to understand more of the ancient world of the Bible.

Bible Anatomy

The Bible is a collection of many different ancient texts, written by many authors, employing a wide variety of forms. It is divided into two main sections, the Old Testament and the New Testament. The Old Testament deals with the history and faith of the Jewish people; the New Testament tells the story of Jesus Christ and the founding of Christianity.

Certain books of the Bible are historical texts that tell their stories in narrative form. The first few books of the Old Testament relate the history of the ancient Jewish people, who are called the Hebrews and the Israelites in different time periods.

These books include the stories of Adam and Eve, Abraham and Sarah, Joseph and his brothers, and many more familiar characters. Several other historical books tell the story of Israel when the nation was ruled by judges and prophets and kings (Judges, Samuel, Kings, and Chronicles).

The first few books in the New Testament are also historical. The four Gospels tell the story of the life of Christ, while the book of Acts recounts the growth of the 1st-century Christian church.

Not all books of the Bible are historical; some of its books consist of prayers and songs, parables and visions. For instance, the book of Psalms in the Old Testament is a collection of songs and poems written out of the experiences of people like King David. The Psalms enlighten us and express deep truths, but they do not tell a narrative story. Some of the books of the New Testament actually consist of the correspondence between early church leaders and the congregations they influenced.

That's one source of the strength of the Bible: Its message is told from the perspectives of individuals and communities of faith, and it reflects their experiences and encounters with the living God. Whether written by a prophet, a king, a female judge, or even a queen, the truth of the Bible flows through specific lives and specific situations. These are stories of God-in-motion, influencing the lives of those who follow him. We often see him most clearly as he is reflected in the responses of those who believed in him.

Bible References

Interspersed throughout the text of this book are references to specific Bible verses. Typically, they list a book, a chapter, and a verse. "John 3:16," for example, refers to the 16th verse of the third chapter of the book of John.

There are 66 different books in the Bible. Some of them are divided into two parts, like 1 Chronicles and 2 Chronicles. In the Old Testament, this often happened for the simple reason that only so much text would fit on one scroll of papyrus or parchment. In the New Testament, some books consist of different letters written to the same recipients, often churches in a certain geographical area, such as the Greek city of Corinth, the subject of the two books, 1 and 2 Corinthians. Most Bibles list the books in the front, both by the order in which they appear and by alphabetical order. So even if you're unfamiliar with the way your Bible is laid out, you can usually find a book easily by page number.

CHAPTER 1

THE DA VINCI CODE

If the mysteries of the Bible seem more mysterious than ever these days, it's due to a single book: Dan Brown's The Da Vinci Code has sold more than 40 million copies in 44 languages since its release in 2003, making it the best-selling novel of all time. Why has it been such a success?

For those who haven't cracked the book yet, here's the premise: A murder in the Louvre and clues in Leonardo da Vinci paintings lead to a secret concerning the relationship between Jesus Christ and Mary Magdalene that has been protected for 2,000 years. If revealed, the novel claims, this explosive revelation could shake the foundations of Christianity, indeed of Western civilization.

In addition to the secret that drives its plot, the thriller offers a host of fascinating puzzles, codes, and clues that wrap the reader in history's mysteries. In Brown's pages secret societies, gnostic gospels, and pagan rites mingle with mathematical puzzles, cryptography, and biblical arcana to keep readers guessing—and turning pages. In addition to generating a cottage industry of debunkers and code breakers online and in print, Brown has been credited with fueling interest in medieval art and church history and boosting tourism in Paris, Rome, and London. As a result, *Time* magazine named him one of the world's most influential people of 2006.

Brown's themes reached an even wider audience when *The Da Vinci Code* reached the big screen. Columbia Pictures' $125 million film, directed by Ron Howard and starring Tom Hanks, was released in May 2006 and quickly became an enormous worldwide success.

Why has *The Da Vinci Code*—which was generally panned by literary critics and laughed at by historians—been so stunningly popular? One reason is society's growing curiosity about all things mystical: Who isn't curious about conspiracy theories, secret societies, and hidden meanings? But what's really boosting sales and challenging churchgoers is the idea that Christianity could conceal a relationship between Jesus and Mary Magdalene for two millennia. So our look at biblical mysteries begins by examining some of *The Da Vinci Code*'s most intriguing theories.

Spoiler warning! The pages that follow might give away some of its clues, so if you haven't already read the book, beware!

The Royal Courts of Justice, London

BROWN ON TRIAL: In 2006 author Dan Brown encountered a plot twist of his own. Writers Michael Baigent and Richard Leigh, authors of *Holy Blood, Holy Grail*, sued Random House, publisher of both their book and *The Da Vinci Code*, in Britain. Their claim: Brown lifted ideas from their 1982 nonfiction work. The case was heard in the Royal Courts of Justice on The Strand, ironically only a short walk from the Temple Church, a key location in *The Da Vinci Code*. In the end, the High Court judge ruled in favor of Dan Brown.

"I worked very hard on this novel, and I certainly expected people would enjoy it, but I never imagined so many people would be enjoying it this much. I wrote this book essentially as a group of fictional characters exploring ideas that I found personally intriguing. These same themes obviously resonate with a great many people." Dan Brown

WAS JESUS

who was **mary magdalene**?

A QUOTE FROM THE BIBLE

LUKE 8:1–2

Soon after this, Jesus was going through towns and villages, telling the good news about God's kingdom. His twelve apostles were with him, and so were some women who had been healed of evil spirits and all sorts of diseases. One of the women was Mary Magdalene, who once had seven demons in her.

MARRIED?

The Bible represents Jesus Christ as the incarnation of God, the Son, who came to Earth to save humanity—not to find a wife.

Was Christ married?

While it's true that the Bible doesn't specifically say Jesus Christ was not married, it does refer to the church, rather than a woman, as his "bride." (See Ephesians 5:22–33.) Yet the idea that Jesus was married has surfaced now and then throughout history in both legends and extra-biblical writings about Mary Magdalene.

One argument for Jesus' being married observes that he lived in a culture that expected men to be married: in fact, ancient Hebrew had no word for *bachelor*. The custom had exceptions, though: members of fringe religious sects like the Essenes, for instance, remained unmarried. However, the Bible describes Jesus as a revolutionary, someone who did not feel compelled to follow cultural dictates—his treatment of the women in his life as equals is an example of his defiance of some social norms of his day.

The Da Vinci Code relies on extrabiblical legends to suggest that Mary Magdalene was Jesus' wife and the mother of his children. Further, it suggests she was also the designated head of the early Christian church, until she was unseated by a jealous apostle Peter. The book also claims that Mary personifies the Sacred Feminine figure worshiped by nature-loving pagans, and that her womb is the true Holy Grail, a title first promulgated by poets of the Middle Ages, who most often used it to denote the cup Jesus allegedly drank from at the Last Supper.

What does the Bible say?

Women were indeed closely involved with Jesus' ministry—it was, after all, a revolutionary one. Mary Magdalene was likely a well-to-do member of an entourage of women who supported and sometimes traveled with Jesus and his disciples.

The Bible teaches that Mary Magdalene, along with some of the other women, was present both at Jesus' death and burial. She was one of the first witnesses to the resurrection and bore the good news back to the cowering disciples—who didn't believe her. She even encountered and spoke with the risen Jesus.

That's the bare essence of Mary of Magdala that can be found in the New Testament. The rest of her story as told in *The Da Vinci Code*—even the familiar notion that she was at one time a prostitute—is based on extrabiblical sources.

A QUOTE FROM THE BIBLE

JOHN 20:11–16

Mary Magdalene stood crying outside the tomb. She was still weeping, when she stooped down and saw two angels inside. They were dressed in white and were sitting where Jesus' body had been. One was at the head and the other was at the foot. The angels asked Mary, "Why are you crying?"

She answered, "They have taken away my Lord's body! I don't know where they have put him." As soon as Mary said this, she turned around and saw Jesus standing there. But she did not know who he was. Jesus asked her, "Why are you crying? Who are you looking for?"

She thought he was the gardener and said, "Sir, if you have taken his body away, please tell me, so I can go and get him."

Then Jesus said to her, "Mary!" She turned and said to him, "Rabboni." The Aramaic word "Rabboni" means "Teacher."

SLANDERED? There is no mention in the Bible that Mary was a reformed prostitute. Pope Gregory the Great first conveyed this misconception in AD 591. The Roman Catholic Church officially refuted it in 1969.

THE SACRED

A key theme in *The Da Vinci Code* is the idea of goddess worship, sometimes called the "Sacred Feminine," and its rejection by the early church. What is the Sacred Feminine? Was it originally part of Christianity?

Religions of the ancient world indeed worshiped multiple gods and goddesses—one of the notable exceptions being the Israelites, who developed a monotheistic religion we know as Judaism. Every culture had its own mythology, usually balancing feminine and masculine. The Egyptians revered Isis and her husband-brother Osiris; Greek mythology honored the god Zeus and his wife Hera; the Roman Pantheon included Jupiter and Juno. The gnostic Christian goddess was named Sophia (wisdom) or Zoe (life). Some believed the Greek goddess Athena to be the feminine counterpart of God the Father.

Some Gnostic teachings claim that true wholeness came from the sacred union between the feminine and masculine. *The Da Vinci Code* advances that theme. In the early church, the special place given to Mary, the mother of Jesus (Acts 1:14), ensured her developing role in Christian theology as a special vehicle of the Holy Spirit (Luke 1:35).

FEMININE

A QUOTE FROM THE BIBLE

GALATIANS 3:26–28

All of you are God's children because of your faith in Christ Jesus. And when you were baptized, it was as though you had put on Christ in the same way you put on new clothes. Faith in Christ Jesus is what makes each of you equal with each other, whether you are a Jew or a Greek, a slave or a free person, a man or a woman.

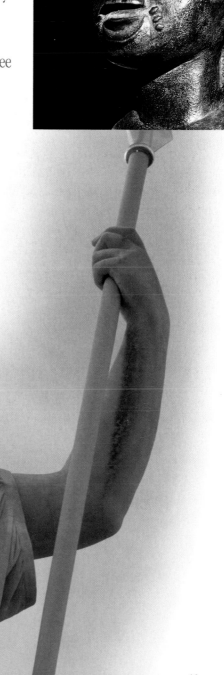

"The sacred feminine is that other face of God that has not been honored over the two millennia of Christianity—at least not as a fully equal partner."

Margaret Starbird, author of *The Woman with the Alabaster Jar: Mary Magdalene and the Holy Grail.*

An antique one-penny coin from the British imperial era, depicting the goddess Britannia.

In this Greek sculpture, a marble and gold covered statue of the greek goddess of wisdom Athena holds the small goddess of victory, Nike, in her hand.

The Da Vinci Code implies that the form of the Bible as we know it was dictated by the Roman Emperor Constantine in the 4th century AD. Constantine, the novel suggests, banned some ancient gospels from his version of the Bible in order to portray Jesus as more godlike and to squelch pagan goddess worship.

Head of Emperor Constantine

The truth is that choosing which ancient documents should make up the canon of Scripture was a process that took the church roughly two centuries. During that time, perhaps at least 50 gospels and writings, such as the *Gospel of Judas*— published for the first time in 2006—were rejected. *The Da Vinci Code* mentions the Nag Hammadi Library, discovered in 1945 in Egypt and published in 1977. This "library" included fourth-century copies like *The Gospel of Mary*, *The Gospel of Philip*, and *The Gospel of Thomas* that were banned by Constantine.

THE BIBLE & GNOSTICISM

What is Gnosticism?

Growing alongside Christianity in the late first and second centuries AD was a philosophy that permeates every plotline in *The Da Vinci Code*, though it is not named outright—Gnosticism.

Gnosticism centers around the idea that gnosis, true knowledge, is secret and understandable only to a chosen few. Gnosticism sees our world, and mankind's place within it, as the residue of dual divinities in conflict. In fact, Gnosticism is dualistic on many levels, pitting eternity versus time, good versus evil, spirit versus matter, and soul versus body.

Influenced by the works of Greek philosopher Plato, Gnosticism argues that the true Christ is not the Jesus who suffered on the cross. It claims that the human substitute called Jesus merely pointed to the real, not-physical Christ. This is in direct contrast to the bedrock principle of mainstream Christianity: that Christ was indeed God made flesh—as, for instance, the apostle John teaches when he writes, "Our ears have heard, our own eyes have seen, and our hands touched this Word [Christ]. The one who gives life appeared!" (1 John 1:1–2).

Through the centuries, Gnosticism has offered a starkly unorthodox way to interpret the Bible and the life of Christ. Once familiar only to biblical scholars, its teachings have been given fresh life for modern readers by *The Da Vinci Code*.

A Quote from Scripture

Many scholars believe that the following words to the Christian church at Colossae refer to Gnosticism:

You died with Christ. Now the forces of the universe don't have any power over you. Why do you live as if you had to obey such rules as, "Don't handle this. Don't taste that. Don't touch this."?

After these things are used, they are no longer good for anything. So why be bothered with the rules that humans have made up?

Obeying these rules may seem to be the smart thing to do. They appear to make you love God more and to be very humble and to have control over your body. But they don't really have any power over our desires.

Colossians 2:20–23

THE PRIORY OF SION AND THE KNIGHTS TEMPLAR

The Priory of Sion, a secret society that drives the plot of *The Da Vinci Code,* never truly existed. Described in the novel as a European order founded in 1099, it was a fantasy created in 1956 by Pierre Plantard, a French anti-Semite with a criminal record for fraud. Plantard claimed to be of Merovingian blood (a French royal line supposedly descending from Jesus and Mary's union). To support his claims, he placed faked documents in France's national library. Thus the Knights Templar couldn't have been founded by the Priory of Sion, as Brown's book claims: the Priory is a hoax!

The Knights Templar, properly known as the Order of the Poor Knights of Christ and the Temple of Solomon, have been shrouded in myth and speculation for centuries. This order of warrior monks was formed to protect pilgrims on their way to the Holy Land, not to to hide documents found under the ruin of Herod's Temple, as Dan Brown suggests in *The Da Vinci Code.*

And yes, the Knights did take a vow of poverty, but their Order became wealthy. Brown portrays the group as a powerful cabal who blackmailed the church, but in fact the Knights Templar amassed their riches through gifts from pilgrims and the sale of relics. They did develop a system of banking, and they did return to Europe—not because they possessed a mysterious treasure, but because all Christians were being forced out of Jerusalem.

The book also claims that the Knights Templar were eventually slaughtered by an irate Pope who was fed up with their greed and subterfuge. This claim is true, in part. On Friday, October 13, 1307, King Philippe IV of France, alarmed by the growing power of the Order, arrested all the Templars in his kingdom—some 2,000 of them. They were tried, convicted, and sentenced to either imprisonment or death. Only about 150 of those convicted were actually Knights; the rest were of a lower order. A sick, weak Pope Clement V was horrified but went along with Philippe's scheme. The brutal episode effectively put an end to the ascendancy of the Knights—and may be the origin of old superstitions about Friday the 13th.

SECRET SOCIETIES

Perhaps the single most memorable character in *The Da Vinci Code* is the albino monk-assassin Silas, who murders the innocent due to his fanatical allegiance to the secretive religious organization Opus Dei. Unlike the entirely fictitious secret society the Priory of Sion, Opus Dei is an actual Roman Catholic organization, but its leaders are quick to note that no Silas-like characters can be found in its ranks. First of all, there are no Opus Dei monks—albino or otherwise. The group is made up predominantly of lay believers, rather than clergy. Second, Opus Dei is not a sect conspiring to protect the Roman Catholic Church from ancient secrets. That doesn't mean, however, that this unusual and secretive organization within Catholicism is free from controversy.

Founded in 1928 by Spanish priest Josémaría Escrivá de Balaguer (1902–1975), left, Opus Dei is not a church, as *The Da Vinci Code* claims. Rather, it is the Roman Catholic Church's only "personal prelature." That means its leaders, or prelates, answer directly to the Pope and have authority over the members of Opus Dei anywhere in the world. The group, which in 2006 numbers more than 80,000 members in 60 countries, is thought to be very rich and influential within its church. Escrivá was canonized in 2002 as a saint by Pope John Paul II, a longtime supporter of Opus Dei.

Critics charge Opus Dei—whose name means God's Work in Latin—with being controlling, aggressive in recruiting practices, and cult-like; they also claim it deliberately splits up families. Opus Dei insists it exists to help Christian laypeople become part of the world by integrating their faith with their daily life, rather than by withdrawing from the world, as some monastic orders do.

In Opus Dei, numeraries—unlike the exaggerated versions in Brown's book—are simply celibate members who live in group-run residences and are closely guided by their spiritual directors. Associate Members are celibate as well, but not residential. Most Opus Dei members are supernumeraries, who are free to have families and own homes. And there are cooperators—nonmember supporters.

Opus Dei members practice corporal mortification—punishing their bodies to maintain spiritual discipline—and that practice adds to the group's mystique. Like the fictional albino monk Silas, an Opus Dei numerary, they do indeed wear a "cilice," a chain with points, for two hours a day, and beat their backs with a small cord once a week while reciting prayer.

Opus Dei members are correct when they point out that corporal mortification is an ancient religious practice that promotes penance and identification with the sufferings of Christ. However, there is no argument that such self-abuse, no matter how principled, seems thoroughly anachronistic to the majority of today's Christians.

DECODING

Dan Brown claims that Leonardo da Vinci was a "known trickster who liked to hide secrets in plain sight." Are Leonardo's paintings actually full of codes? Most art scholars say no. And contrary to the book, Leonardo's output wasn't prolific; by comparison to his peers it was notoriously meager.

LEONARDO

"The Last Supper"

The iconic "The Last Supper," painted on a wall in the convent of Santa Maria delle Grazie in Milan, plays a key role in *The Da Vinci Code*. Leonardo shows Jesus surrounded by his apostles, as his notes and sketches from the time indicate. Yet Brown claims the figure on Jesus' right is actually Mary Magdalene, in a position that conveys her special relationship to Christ. Historically that figure is interpreted as St. John the Evangelist, thought to be the youngest of the apostles and often pictured in medieval art without a beard. It was the custom to depict young men in Florentine art in an androgynous or effeminate manner, a detail overlooked by Brown. Moreover, if that figure is Mary Magdalene, where is John?

And that floating dagger, which Brown suggests is a symbol? It belongs to Peter, perhaps suggesting his impulsive use of a dagger to slice a guard's ear in the Garden of Gethsemane when Jesus was arrested (John 18:10).

And Peter's hand at John/Mary's throat? Is it really threatening him/her—or is it simply what it appears to be—an attempt to get his/her attention?

"Madonna of the Rocks"

Why did Leonardo paint two versions of this image of the Madonna? Brown claims the second version was created because the first one alarmed Roman Catholic leaders by giving too much power to the goddess figure. Many purport that the second stays truer to the biblical narrative, while the original version does not. Interestingly, in Brown's story, cryptologist Sophie Neveu bends the painting to retrieve a key taped on its back. The actual piece, however, is made of wood and stands six feet tall.

"Mona Lisa"

What about the world's most famous painting, the "Mona Lisa"? Is she Leonardo in drag? A subtle message of the preeminence of androgyny? Her enigmatic smile gives nothing away.

At least that part of Brown's story is true to reality.

"[*The Da Vinci Code*] ... would not be worth refuting if there were not the danger—now there is so much less knowledge of Christian history than in the past—that some people may be seduced into believing or half-believing it."

Reverend Dr. Nicholas Sagovsky, Canon Theologian of Westminster Abbey, London, England, in a sermon on October 31, 2004.

the wonders of
creation

CHAPTER

2

April showers fall to earth, and a rainbow blooms in the eastern sky. Some of the rainwater runs to the sea; some is drawn up by the heat of the sun and transformed into vapor, forming towering rain clouds. And the cycle of life begins again. The mysteries of our world are so close to us, so much a part of our every waking moment, that we can run the risk of taking these marvels for granted. Yet who has not wondered, What force shaped the vast, complex web of life around us? What mechanism holds the

"Would it not be strange if a universe without purpose accidentally created humans who are so obsessed with purpose?"

Sir John Templeton,
The Humble Approach: Scientists Discover God

forces of nature in perfect balance—or unleashes them in the form of natural disasters? And how do we answer the most basic question of all— where did these wonders and marvels come from?

The Bible's answer is clear: our universe in all its splendor, our world and all its wonders, our human bodies and all their complicated parts . . . all this vast yet intricate creation sprang from one source—from an intelligent being operating with a deliberate design—the mind and hand of God.

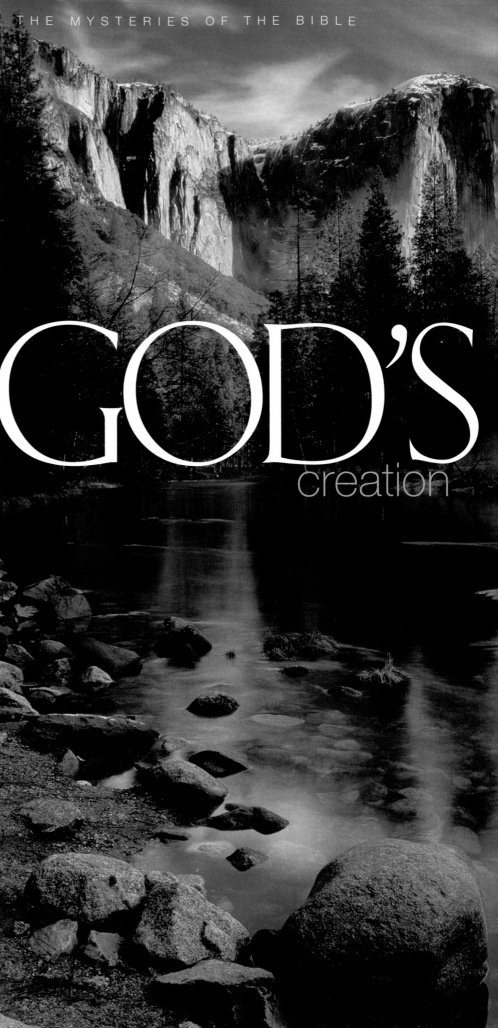

GOD'S creation

A QUOTE FROM THE BIBLE

PSALM 8:3–4

I often think of the heavens your hands have made, and of the moon and stars you put in place. Then I ask, "Why do you care about us humans? Why are you concerned for us weaklings?"

"A common-sense and satisfying interpretation of our world suggests the designing hand of a super intelligence."

— Owen Gingerich, senior astronomer at the Smithsonian Astrophysical Observatory, "Dare a Scientist Believe in Design?" in *Evidence of Purpose*

"I do not believe that any scientists who examined the evidence would fail to draw the inference that the laws of nuclear physics have been deliberately designed with regard to the consequences they produce inside stars."

— Sir Fred Hoyle, *Annual Review of Astronomy and Astrophysics*

"A universe aiming at the production of man implies a mind directing it. Though man is not at the physical center of the universe, he appears to be at the center of its purpose."

— Robert M. Augros and George N. Stanciu, *The New Story of Science*

"It is hard to resist the impression that the present structure of the universe, apparently so sensitive to minor alterations in numbers, has been rather carefully thought out . . . The seemingly miraculous concurrence of these numerical values must remain the most compelling evidence for cosmic design."

— Paul Davies, *The Cosmic Blueprint: New Discoveries in Nature's Creative Ability to Order the Universe*

A QUOTE FROM THE BIBLE

ISAIAH 45:18

The LORD alone is God!
He created the heavens
and made a world
where people can live,
instead of creating
an empty desert.
The LORD alone is God;
there are no others.

Source: *The Case for a Creator* written by Lee Strobel (2004, Zondervan).

25

1 2 3 4 5 6 7

days of **creation**

The best-known biblical account of creation can be found in Genesis 1, the opening chapter of the Bible. A second, different account of creation appears in Genesis 2.

In Genesis 1, God speaks the earth and its inhabitants into being. A different layer of life appears each day, until on the sixth day, humankind is given the power to enjoy and to care for our world.

The origin of this miraculous world in which we live—no matter how we describe God's process in our modern words and ideas—is a mystery and a wonder. Yet, even as in the time of Adam and Eve, this world remains both our gift— and our responsibility.

IN THE BEGINNING GOD CREATED THE HEAVENS AND THE EARTH

DAY 1

GOD SAID, "I command light to shine!" And light started shining. God … named the light "Day" and the darkness "Night"… that was the first day.

DAY 2

GOD SAID, "I command a dome to separate the water above it from the water below it." And that's what happened. God … named it "Sky" … that was the second day.

DAY 3

GOD SAID, "I command the water under the sky to come together in one place, so there will be dry ground" … God named the dry ground "Land," and he named the water "Ocean"… God said, "I command the earth to produce all kinds of plants, including fruit trees and grain." And that's what happened … that was the third day.

DAY 4

GOD SAID, "I command lights to appear in the sky and to separate day from night and to show the time for seasons, special days, and years …" God made two powerful lights, the brighter one to rule the day and the other to rule the night. He also made the stars … that was the fourth day.

DAY 5

GOD SAID, "I command the ocean to be full of living creatures, and I command birds to fly above the earth." So God made the giant sea monsters and all the living creatures that swim in the ocean. He also made every kind of bird … that was the fifth day.

DAY 6

GOD SAID, "I command the earth to give life to all kinds of tame animals, wild animals, and reptiles"… God said, "Now we will make humans, and they will be like us. We will let them rule the fish, the birds, and all other living creatures." So God created … men and women … that was the sixth day.

DAY 7

So the heavens and the earth and everything else were created. By the seventh day God had finished his work, and so he rested. God blessed the seventh day and made it special.

Adapted from Genesis 1:1–2:3

the moon

The fact that our universe works is a marvel in itself: it is a masterpiece of balance and proportion, of many disparate forces working as one. The complexity of the mechanics and the simplicity of the effect—the breeze on our faces, the sound of the waves—point to the Creator described in the Bible. On any clear night or day, look up in the sky—you'll find a mystery in plain view.

and the sun

The Moon

You don't have to believe in the man-in-the-moon to find our closest neighbor in space is an enigma and a riddle, for the moon plays a mystifying role in our lives on earth. Most importantly, from 250,000 miles away, it regulates our seasons by stabilizing the tilt of the earth's axis. Imagine our world without it: Instead of a one and a half-degree tilt, the earth might swing like an off-kilter pendulum, its temperature and climate as erratic as its trajectory.

The moon also plays an important role with the sun in controlling the tides. Let their balance go awry, and the oceans of the earth could surge and slosh like bathtub water at the mercy of a playful child. In short, the moon keeps the earth inhabitable for us. It's one wonder we can all too easily take for granted.

The Sun

Earth's sun is a star—the star closest to us and thus the brightest star that we see. In fact, it makes up 98 percent of the mass of our solar system (more than one million earths could fit in the sun). The temperature at the sun's core can be as much as 27,000,000 degrees Fahrenheit. Unlike our planet, the sun is not made up of hard matter. Instead, it is a constantly revolving ball of erupting gas, mostly hydrogen and helium.

Of all the mysteries built into the delicate mechanism of our universe, one of the greatest is the precision of the distance between the earth and the sun—it is perfectly balanced to support human life. Closer, and it would be impossible to keep water on our planet from evaporating or even boiling away. Farther, and earth's water would freeze solid.

only

"You are the one who put me together inside my mother's body, and I praise you because of the wonderful way you created me.

A QUOTE FROM THE BIBLE

GENESIS 1:26–28

God said, "Now we will make humans, and they will be like us. We will let them rule the fish, the birds, and all other living creatures." So God created humans to be like himself; he made men and women. God gave them his blessing and said: Have a lot of children! Fill the earth with people and bring it under your control. Rule over the fish in the ocean, the birds in the sky, and every animal on the earth.

As Genesis 1 describes it, God created humans, men and women, on the sixth day of creation. Just as nature reveals a variety of designs that work together to sustain life, the human body, on close inspection, reveals a host of intricate systems working in unison to keep us alive. We need look no further than our own hands—with our own eyes—to experience the mystery of God's creative design.

human?

Everything you do is marvelous! Of this I have no doubt." Psalm 139:13–14

Our Amazing Bodies

The adult human body is made up of 206 bones that provide its structure. Those bones are covered by twice as many muscles, without which the bones couldn't move. The body has systems to help us breathe, to circulate our blood, digest our food, and even heal ourselves when we are injured. We wear our largest organ of all on the outside—our skin. Most adults have at least 20 square feet of the stuff. It's waterproof, self-repairing, and it constantly renews and sheds itself.

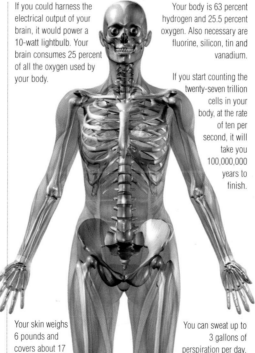

If you could harness the electrical output of your brain, it would power a 10-watt lightbulb. Your brain consumes 25 percent of all the oxygen used by your body.

Your body is 63 percent hydrogen and 25.5 percent oxygen. Also necessary are fluorine, silicon, tin and vanadium.

If you start counting the twenty-seven trillion cells in your body, at the rate of ten per second, it will take you 100,000,000 years to finish.

Your body is creating and killing 15 million red blood cells per second.

A drop of human blood contains about 250 million cells. One square inch of a hand contains about 1,300 nerve endings. For our whole lives, our hearts don't rest for more than a second.

Your skin weighs 6 pounds and covers about 17 square feet.

You can sweat up to 3 gallons of perspiration per day.

The eye is essentially an opaque eyeball filled with a water-like fluid.

One out of every 100 cells in our body works to defend us against disease. So if you weigh 150 pounds, 1¹/₂ pounds of you are for self-defense.

Fingerprints are our built-in, easily accessible identity cards. They are a unique marker for a person, even for two otherwise identical twins.

CHAPTER 3

mysterious

Its message stronger than the passage of time, the Bible still speaks to us thousands of years after it was written. Yet more than the great book's pages still endure: it's possible today to actually walk through the same towns and streets where David and Solomon, Jesus and Peter once walked. The city of Jerusalem still stands in the Middle East—and appears all too often in our living rooms on the evening news. We can visit the city of Jericho, where Joshua's trumpets once made the walls come tumbling down. We can stand on the shores of the Sea of Galilee, where Christ walked upon the water. We can swim in the Mediterranean, but keep your eyes peeled!—for that's where Jonah was swallowed by a mighty fish.

But not all the significant places and artifacts mentioned in the Bible have survived. And while scholars and archaeologists scour libraries and probe the desert sands for shreds of information to confirm what people in biblical times saw and experienced, they don't always find what they're looking for.

disappearances

As in the classic film *Raiders of the Lost Ark,* in which gutsy archaeologist Indiana Jones battles Nazi generals as they vie to locate the resting place of the Hebrews' sacred Ark of the Covenant, scholars still dream of locating the Garden of Eden or the remains of the Tower of Babel—or even, perhaps, the fossilized horn of a unicorn— missing links that can bring people and places apparently long lost to antiquity back to fresh life.

the garden of eden

Imagine a bright green rainforest, lush with flowers and fruit, at the dawn of history, where the very first man and woman ever created lived in perfect peace with animals, plants, the weather—and their Creator. This, the Bible tells us in its first book, Genesis, was the Garden of Eden, humankind's first home and a paradise of earthly delight. (In fact, the word Eden is derived from the Hebrew word for delight.) Yet this first couple, Adam and Eve, were no more perfect than are we: guilty of yielding to temptation, they were expelled from the garden by a God who was sadly disappointed in his new creatures.

A QUOTE FROM THE BIBLE
GENESIS 2:8–15

The LORD made a garden in a place called Eden, which was in the east, and he put the man there. The LORD God placed all kinds of beautiful trees and fruit trees in the garden. Two other trees were in the middle of the garden. One of the trees gave life—the other gave the power to know the difference between right and wrong.

From Eden a river flowed out to water the garden, then it divided into four rivers. The first one is the Pishon River that flows through the land of Havilah, where pure gold, rare perfumes, and precious stones are found. The second is the Gihon River that winds through Ethiopia. The Tigris River that flows east of Assyria is the third, and the fourth is the Euphrates River. The LORD God put the man in the Garden of Eden to take care of it and to look after it.

In Search of the Lost Garden

All the Bible offers as to the garden's location is found in Genesis 2:8–15: It was planted to the east, in Eden. From it, one unnamed river flowed and divided into four new rivers: Pishon, Gihon, Tigris, and Euphrates. The first two of these rivers have no known modern counterparts, and their locations are purely speculative. While both the Tigris and Euphrates rivers exist today, many factors—including possible changes in their courses over the centuries—make it very difficult to pinpoint Eden's location today.

So what became of this idyllic place? Genesis 3 reveals these facts: After defying God by eating of the fruit he forbade them (which scholars now think probably wasn't an apple), Adam and Eve were banished from the garden. An angel was assigned to guard the entrance to keep anyone from entering. Because of this, Adam and Eve were the only humans ever to enjoy the Garden of Eden.

A bas-relief sculpture of Adam and Eve's tree.

Back to the Garden

In his book, *Paradise Found*, published in 1885, Rev. Dr. William F. Warren posited that the North Pole was the site of the garden of Eden. Joseph Smith, the founder of the Mormon Church, believed that Eden was in Missouri. Baptist minister Elvy E. Callaway believed that Bristol, Florida, was the place. (His reasoning was that the area has a four-headed river system, as well as growths of gopher wood, the wood Noah used to build the ark.) Most scholars believe the Garden of Eden was located somewhere in the vicinity of Egypt, Iraq, India, Ethiopia, or Sudan. A 1996 satellite photo of the area showed a channel, now dry, connecting an area near the Red Sea to Kuwait. Some scholars speculated that this long-dry channel could have been the Pishon River.

So, with the technology available to us today, why can't we pinpoint Eden's location? Some scholars believe that the garden fell victim to the destructive flood of Noah's day, which swamped the entire world. Others believe that global climate changes, even before the flood, could have helped obscure its location. Because the Bible mentions only a garden, and no associated man-made structures that might have survived over thousands of years, we may never know where this earthly paradise was located. Yet somewhere in the fabric of humanity is a yearning to return to a place where we have what we need and no person subjugates another to survive. As Joni Mitchell wrote in her utopian song *Woodstock:* "We've got to get ourselves back to the garden."

noah's ark

Noah's Ark—the vast vessel that floats at the center of a story shared by Jews, Christians, and Muslims—is one of the most familiar images in the world, despite the many different ways artists have portrayed it. In children's stories, it's often a round-bellied boat bobbing on the sea, with knobby-headed giraffes and plush lions peering from its windows, all framed by a cheery rainbow. But is the ark a myth, or did it really exist? And if so, what did it really look like—and where did it go? And the story that Noah saved the animals so the world could be re-created—is it possible? Or preposterous?

The Dimensions

The mystery of Noah's Ark begins with its specifications, precisely listed in the Bible: It was 300 cubits long, 50 cubits wide, and 30 cubits high. That's a seaworthy 450 feet x 75 feet x 45 feet, for one cubit measures around 18 inches. The vessel was made of gopher wood—possibly cypress or cedar. A row of small windows crowned its three decks. There was one big door —and no emergency exits!

The ark's exact shape is unknown, of course. Most scholars say it likely resembled a large barge. Into this ancient cargo ship Noah and his family loaded mammals, birds, reptiles, and inverte- brates in twos and sevens for a long, fantastic voyage. After five months, the Bible says, the ark landed "somewhere in the Ararat mountains."

Ark Chasers

Many cultures tell stories of a great primeval flood. One well-known example is the Sumerian "Epic of Gilgamesh," written sometime between 1300 BC and 1000 BC. Yet in other religious traditions, Noah's Ark isn't the object of fascination it is for Christianity. And much of the scientific community has had little to do with the search for the ark, assuming a wooden vessel could not have survived many millennia of exposure.

Nevertheless, numerous alleged sightings of the ark in the modern era have fueled speculation, prompted hundreds of Indiana Jones- style expeditions, and created a small industry of ark hunters and their supporters. Among them was the late American astronaut James Irwin, who combed most of Mt. Ararat on foot and then surveyed and photographed it from the air.

Room on Board?

How could thousands of animals have fit into the ark? First of all, remember that there was no need to include aquatic creatures. That con- sideration leaves the estimated tally of animals at around 16,000. Scholars also point out that if Noah included two of every kind of animal, that needn't mean two of every breed.

According to the specs we do have, some estimate the ark's floor space as 100,000 sq. ft. (that's over one million cubic feet). That would mean the ark could have held as many animals as almost 600 rail- road cars (almost 130 sheep can fit into a single-decker sheep car). Noah might have played ringmaster to an enormous sailing circus. If the animals Noah picked were young, thus smaller, perhaps he just managed to squeeze them all in—as long as no one exhaled!

Mt. Ararat? Where's That At?

A volcano and one of the tallest mountains in the Middle East, modern-day Mt. Ararat, in Eastern Turkey, is the most popular site for modern ark-hunters. It's so mammoth, it has a permanent ice cap, which could conceal an ancient artifact like the ark.

On the other hand, some scholars believe the Bible may have been referring not to Mt. Ararat, but rather to Urartu, an ancient kingdom in this mountainous region.

Durupinar, a canoe-shaped formation named for the Turkish captain who discovered it 18 miles south of Greater Ararat, is another site.

Another school of thought focuses on Al Judi, also known as Mount Cudi, a peak in southeastern Turkey.

And some ark-hunters have suggested that Ethiopia and even Ireland are possible locations for the site of the ancient vessel.

What exactly is Mt. Sinai? Since Sinai can refer to both a desert and a mountain, the discussion can get a little confusing. It doesn't help that the Israelites also referred to Sinai by alternate names, such as Mt. Horeb and the Desert of Sin. (Sin, in this case, doesn't refer to misdeeds, but to an ancient god of nomads. Sinai may be an alternate form of Sin.) According to Exodus, the second book of the Bible, Mt. Sinai is where God gave Moses the Ten Commandments. It was the first major campsite for the Hebrews after they escaped their bondage as a nation of slaves in Egypt.

mt. sinai

The location of the desert of Sinai, where the Israelites wandered for 40 years, is not a mystery. Sinai is the peninsula between Egypt and Saudi Arabia; it lies just beneath Jordan. The peninsula is shaped like an upside-down pyramid in between the two legs of the Red Sea, the Gulf of Suez and the Gulf of Aqaba.

On the other hand, the exact location of the biblical Mt. Sinai is indeed a mystery. Many believe it to be Jebel Musa (7,500 ft.), one of three tall granite peaks that rises in the Sinai Desert. It is now the location of St. Catherine's Monastery, which holds what is considered one of the richest libraries of sacred manuscripts and scrolls in the world. In the 4th century AD, long before the monastery was built, the Church of the Burning Bush was built upon this location.

Other places considered as possible locations of Mt. Sinai—including some scholars' favorite, Mt. Ras es-Safsafeh—lie to the north and east of Jebel Musa.

THE TEN COMMANDMENTS

I

God said to the people of Israel: I am the LORD your God, the one who brought you out of Egypt where you were slaves. Do not worship any god except me.

II

Do not make idols that look like anything in the sky or on earth or in the ocean under the earth. Don't bow down and worship idols. I am the LORD your God, and I demand all your love.

III

Do not misuse my name. I am the LORD your God, and I will punish anyone who misuses my name.

IV

Remember that the Sabbath Day belongs to me. You have six days when you can do your work, but the seventh day of each week belongs to me, your God. No one is to work on that day—not you, your children, your slaves, your animals, or the foreigners who live in your towns.

V

Respect your father and your mother, and you will live a long time in the land I am giving you.

VI

Do not murder.

VII

Be faithful in marriage.

VIII

Do not steal.

IX

Do not tell lies about others.

X

Do not want anything that belongs to someone else. Don't want anyone's house, wife or husband, slaves, oxen, donkeys or anything else.

~Adapted from Exodus 20:1–7
Note: Various faith traditions number the Ten Commandments differently.

Why Is Sinai So Important?

Mt. Sinai was the place where God revealed his presence to the Hebrew people through their leader, Moses. While Moses met God on the mountain, the tribes of Israel watched from below, and Sinai's slopes were covered in thick, dark smoke. Suddenly trumpets blasted loudly, thunder rumbled and lightning flashed, terrifying the onlookers. The word went out: while God was meeting with Moses, any person or living thing that tried to come up the mountain, or even touch it, would be put to death.

Moses spent forty days and nights in God's presence. This was when the Ten Commandments were written; the Bible tells us they were carved into tablets of stone by the hand of God himself.

dinosaurs

The Bible teems with interesting creatures. There are mentions of giants, dragons, and multi-headed creatures, among others. But if these critters were real, where are they now? And what about dinosaurs? Why aren't the "terrible lizards" mentioned in the Bible? The first reason is a practical one. The word dinosaur wasn't coined until the mid-1800s AD. The Bible as we know it was finished late in the 1st century AD, and not translated into English until the 1300s. So if you are looking for the word dinosaur in the Bible, it naturally won't appear.

Of the animals mentioned in the Bible, some of the more bizarre creatures appear in books like Isaiah and Revelation. Unlike the books of the Bible that tell of the history of the Hebrews or the life of Christ, these other books describe future events like the apocalypse that will end our world and herald Christ's return, or even otherworldly events glimpsed in religious trances. Much of their narratives are visions, one writer's attempt to describe something no one on earth has ever seen, and which have no earthly counterpart.

In other cases, writers of the Bible were describing real animals, but shifts in language and meaning affected the translation process from ancient languages into modern English, sowing confusion. Here are three creatures mentioned in the Bible that don't seem to have any contemporary counterparts . . . or do they?

Leviathan

This creature is described in the 41st chapter of the book of Job, the story of a wealthy man who lost everything. Some say Job is talking about a crocodile. Yet he says this beast sneezes lightning (v. 18), spits sparks and fire (v. 19), blows smoke out its nose (v. 20), and has blazing breath (v. 21). Modern translations generally depict the Leviathan as a sea monster. Was this enormous creature real or is it merely a metaphor? Was it a dinosaur? A crocodile? A whale? You decide!

Behemoth

Before Leviathan, Job also mentioned a Behemoth (Job 40:15). Modern versions of the Bible generally translate this word as referring to the hippopotamus, an animal that was well known in ancient Egypt. Today we still find hippopotamuses (or hippopotami, if you prefer) in Africa, but there is also fossil evidence that they existed in northern Galilee and the Jordan Valley.

A word similar to Behemoth is used in other books of the Bible (Deuteronomy 28:26; 32:24; Isaiah 18:6, and Habakkuk 2:17), but it has most often been translated simply as "beast." Some scholars believe that in these cases, the term refers to elephants or rhinoceroses. But no matter what you call it, one thing's for sure: this beast was big, powerful, and intimidating.

Unicorns

In the most famous of the early English Bible translations, the King James Version, there are nine references to unicorns: Numbers 23:22; 24:8; Deuteronomy 33:17; Job 39:9–10; Psalms 22:21; 29:6; 92:10; Isaiah 34:7. More recent versions often translate the word as wild-ox. How, you may wonder, could an ox be confused with a unicorn? Here's where the language issue comes into play. One view is that these unicorns were actually the Arabian oryx (a sort of ox-antelope) which has two nearly straight horns in its head. Often these horns were as long as the animal's head, and sometimes they grew so large they could hold up to four gallons of liquid—in fact, the ancient Israelites used oryx horns as goblets.

Truthfully, in the context of the passages where the word unicorn appears, "ox" makes much more sense. Perhaps the use of the term was a romantic, early 1600s translation of the original Hebrew. We've looked, but we can't find any evidence that the original word implied an animal with only a single horn. Sorry, unicorn-lovers!

So . . . the Bible speaks of the Leviathan, the Behemoth, and the unicorn. And not a dinosaur among them!

A QUOTE FROM THE BIBLE

JOB 41:1–29

Can you catch a sea monster by using a fishhook? Can you tie its mouth shut with a rope? Can it be led around by a ring in its nose or a hook in its jaw? Will it beg for mercy? Will it surrender as a slave for life? Can it be tied by the leg like a pet bird for little girls? Is it ever chopped up and its pieces bargained for in the fish-market? Can it be killed with harpoons or spears? Wrestle it just once—that will be the end. Merely a glimpse of this monster makes all courage melt. And if it is too fierce for anyone to attack, who would dare oppose me? I am in command of the world and in debt to no one.

What powerful legs, what a stout body this monster possesses! Who could strip off its armor or bring it under control with a harness? Who would try to open its jaws, full of fearsome teeth? Its back is covered with shield after shield, firmly bound and closer together than breath to breath.

When this monster sneezes, lightning flashes, and its eyes glow like the dawn. Sparks and fiery flames explode from its mouth. And smoke spews from its nose like steam from a boiling pot, while its blazing breath scorches everything in sight.

Its neck is so tremendous that everyone trembles, the weakest parts of its body are harder than iron, and its heart is stone. When this noisy monster appears, even the most powerful turn and run in fear. No sword or spear can harm it, and weapons of bronze or iron are as useless as straw or rotten wood. Rocks thrown from a sling cause it no more harm than husks of grain. This monster fears no arrows, it simply smiles at spears, and striking it with a stick is like slapping it with straw.

the tower of babel

A QUOTE FROM THE BIBLE
GENESIS 11:1–9

Few acts of humanity's defiance of the Creator can match the brazenness of the building of the world's first skyscraper, the tower we now refer to as Babel. Here's how the story began: God directed men and women to fill the earth by scattering themselves across it. Humans had a different idea, though: they chose to cluster together in large cities.

Emboldened by a mob mentality, many Babylonians sought to rival God's power. Their quest was to reach the heavens themselves, via a spire magnificent enough to enter God's realm. One key to the collaborative building effort was the fact that every worker on the tower—everyone in the known world—spoke the same language and thus could communicate easily.

A disappointed, angry God foiled the plan. According to the book of Genesis, God issued new languages to the workers, and people began speaking words they had never heard before. They found themselves unable to understand friends and neighbors they had talked with for years. Language became gibberish, collaboration turned to confusion—and the tower fell.

At first everyone spoke the same language, but after some of them moved from the east and settled in Babylonia, they said: Let's build a city with a tower that reaches to the sky! We'll use hard bricks and tar instead of stone and mortar. We'll become famous, and we won't be scattered all over the world.

But when the LORD came down to look at the city and the tower, he said:

These people are working together because they all speak the same language. This is just the beginning. Soon they will be able to do anything they want. Come on! Let's go down and confuse them by making them speak different languages—then they won't be able to understand each other.

So the people had to stop building the city, because the LORD confused their language and scattered them all over the earth. That's how the city of Babel got its name.

Where Is It Now?

While the Tower of Babel is long gone, the city in which it was built has maintained a prominent profile throughout history. On Old Testament maps, Babylon can be found roughly 500 miles east of Jerusalem, between the Tigris and Euphrates rivers. Today that land is part of Iraq.

Genesis 10–11 contains the first biblical references to Babylon, but certainly not the last. The city and its people are cast as villains—thorns in the side of the Israelites—throughout the Old Testament. The word Babylon itself became synonymous with wickedness and ungodliness. In the New Testament, John, the author of Revelation, used the name *Babylon* as a way of secretly identifying the Christian church's biggest foe in his day—the powerful city of Rome.

Some consider the Tower of Babel to be the first of the pyramids, although it probably didn't resemble the familiar pyramids of Egypt, but rather the ziggurats of Mesopotamia. Rather than the sloping sides of the pyramids, ziggurats have layered, stepped sides, which we can still see in the Choqa Zanbil in western Iran. After its builders scattered, the Tower of Babel became known as the Temple of Belus. Here's a description of it, written in 1836 by George Jones: "This temple was square, measuring at its base 660 feet on each side; and consisted of eight successive layers or towers, formed of huge unburnt bricks, each layer 75 feet high, and each smaller than the next below. It was thus altogether 600 [feet] in height, and had

stairway to heaven

on the summit a chapel for the golden statue of their god. According to Diodorus Siculus, the gold of this statue, and the decorations of the temple, were equal in value to 100 million dollars while the worth of the utensils employed, and the treasure deposited here, amounted to an equal sum." Jones believed that the people of Babel had been so awed by the supernatural work of God in scrambling their languages that the actual tower came to represent that awesome power, and so they adopted the structure of the Tower of Babel in other temples built for their mysterious deities.

the ark of the covenant

The Ark of the Covenant was, in the simplest terms, a piece of furniture, an ornate chest placed in the innermost chamber of the tabernacle, the portable temple used by the Hebrews as they wandered in the desert on their journey to the land of Canaan. The ark was crafted to house the stone tablets of the Ten Commandments; later it was placed in a special chamber in Solomon's Temple in Jerusalem.

The innermost chambers of both the traveling tabernacle and Solomon's Temple were shrouded in significance and secrecy. They were seen by the ancient Israelites as the exact place where God actually lived among them. Other sacred artifacts—Aaron's miraculous staff that budded with new blossoms even after being cut, and the wondrous manna the Hebrews ate on their journey— were placed with great ceremony within the Ark of the Covenant over the years.

Search for the Holy Grail

Like the Ark of the Covenant, the Holy Grail has inspired quests through the centuries; it is still an object of allure today. Knights of King Arthur's legendary Round Table frequently set out in search of the grail, as parodied in the 1975 movie satire *Monty Python and the Holy Grail*. In the movie *Indiana Jones and the Last Crusade*, the grail was characterized as a chalice that could imbue eternal life to those who drank from it. While we most often think of the grail as a cup or bowl that was believed to have been used by Jesus at the Last Supper, many legends outside of standard church teaching include other definitions of the grail, but in each case the grail represents an object somehow endowed with special powers or God's favor.

The Holy Grail is often associated with Joseph of Arimathaea, the wealthy man of the New Testament who loaned a tomb for the burial of Jesus. Some believe Joseph took the grail to England in AD 63 when he traveled there to spread the gospel. Through the dark medieval years of the church, Joseph's grail represented a spiritual authority outside of the Roman Catholic Church, and added fuel to the fiery political and religious conflicts of that day.

The truth is, there is not one direct biblical reference to the Holy Grail; its existence has never been anything but purely speculative. The first references to the Grail are found in the works of medieval French poets who lived long after the Bible was written. The novel *The Da Vinci Code* has popularized an even more fanciful idea: that the Holy Grail represents the womb of the wife of Christ himself. Since it is entirely fictional in the first place, the concept of the Holy Grail will no doubt generate more such unbiblical notions and more unsuccessful quests. Legends surrounding a mysterious ancient religious relic are romantic, it's true, but the profound—and very real— teachings that Jesus offered the world hold far more significance.

Can't Touch This!

Like Mt. Sinai when God was present, the ark was considered untouchable. In fact, there were extensive instructions given about how to carry the ark as the people traveled: They used special poles that slid through loops attached to the ark, and it was borne only by Levitical priests.

The Bible records several instances in which people failed to honor the no-touch zone. The Philistines, longtime enemies of the Hebrews, once captured the ark— only to find the cities where they stashed it suffered wild afflictions; some of the people died just looking inside the chest.

In fact, the Philistines passed the ark around like a hot potato until they finally, desperately, sent it back home (1 Samuel 5–7). Later, during the famous King David's reign, an attempt was made to transport the ark to Jerusalem on a cart, rather than by the poles designed to carry it. When the cart hit a bump, a man who was not a Levite reached out to steady it—and was immediately struck dead (1 Chronicles 13).

While the movie *Raiders of the Lost Ark* portrayed the power inherent in the ancient Ark of the Covenant, it also indicated that the chest is now stored in some obscure and forgotten corner of a U.S. government warehouse. There's no evidence to support this obviously fictional story. The original ark no longer exists.

As far as we know, that is.

manna

Manna? What's that? This was the question the Hebrews asked when they first saw the mysterious substance that fell from the sky and became their sustenance during their long wanderings in the desert of Sinai. In fact, the name manna may actually be a transliteration of the question "What is it?" Or it may be derived from the Egyptian word for food, mennu.

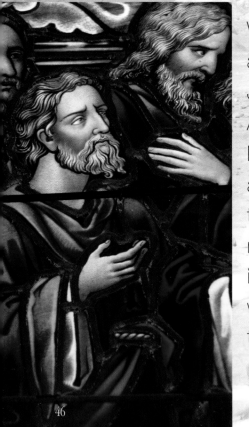

What was manna? Even today, no one knows the answer: it remains a mystery, and to some in the Jewish, Islamic, and Christian traditions, it is a miracle. According to the Old Testament books Exodus and Numbers, manna would come with the evening dew and melt in the morning sun. Every day for 40 years the Israelites gathered this whitish substance that resembled coriander seed, then ground or crushed it into an aromatic resin similar to myrrh. Then they would boil or bake it into wafers. The Bible tells us it tasted as if it were made with honey or sweet olive oil.

Scholars speculate that manna may have been a type of lichen, or was related to the juice of various plants after it dried and flaked. Another theory is that manna was the crystallized secretion of insects that fed on twigs from the tamarisk tree. But these substances, which sound less than appetizing to begin with, cannot be crushed and boiled as the manna was, and they certainly weren't nutritious enough to sustain thousands of people over four decades.

And if manna occurred naturally in the Holy Land, why did the Israelites not recognize it when they first saw it, as the Bible notes? And why didn't other cultures cultivate it?

Other mysteries surrounded the manna. For one thing, it appeared on six days, but never on the Sabbath, the Hebrews' weekly holy day of rest. And however many omers of manna (between six and seven pints) each family collected, the amount was exactly what they needed for that day. Nor could they hoard it—any extra manna would turn putrid the next day. But to prepare for the Sabbath, the people collected twice as much manna and it stayed fresh for two days. This supernatural rationing system continued until the Israelites crossed the Jordan River, reached the Promised Land, and began to eat the grain grown there—then the manna stopped.

As a kind of souvenir or relic, God had the high priest put an omer of manna in the Ark of the Covenant. What became of that omer of manna is, of course, another mystery.

Exodus 16:14–26

After the dew had gone, the desert was covered with thin flakes that looked like frost. The people had never seen anything like this, and they started asking each other, "What is it?" Moses answered, "This is the bread that the LORD has given you to eat. And he orders you to gather about two quarts for each person in your family—that should be more than enough."

They did as they were told. Some gathered more and some gathered less, according to their needs, and none was left over.

Moses told them not to keep any overnight. Some of them disobeyed, but the next morning what they kept was stinking and full of worms, and Moses was angry.

Each morning everyone gathered as much as they needed, and in the heat of the day the rest melted. However, on the sixth day of the week, everyone gathered enough to have four quarts, instead of two. When the leaders reported this to Moses, he told them that the LORD had said, "Tomorrow is the Sabbath, a sacred day of rest in honor of me. So gather all you want to bake or boil, and make sure you save enough for tomorrow."

The people obeyed, and the next morning the food smelled fine and had no worms. "You may eat the food," Moses said. "Today is the Sabbath in honor of the LORD, and there won't be any of this food on the ground today. You will find it there for the first six days of the week, but not on the Sabbath."

Jesus used manna to explain himself to his followers:

"For example, when our ancestors were in the desert, they were given manna to eat. It happened just as the Scriptures say, 'God gave them bread from heaven to eat.'" Jesus then told them, "I tell you for certain that Moses wasn't the one who gave you bread from heaven. My Father is the one who gives you the true bread from heaven. And the bread that God gives is the one who came down from heaven to give life to the world . . . I am the bread that gives life! Your ancestors ate manna in the desert, and later they died. But the bread from heaven has come down, so that no one who eats it will ever die. I am that bread from heaven! Everyone who eats it will live forever. My flesh is the life-giving bread that I give to the people of this world." (John 6:31–33; 48–51).

The More Things Change . . .

The world of the ancients seems foreign in many ways from our modern world. But through the ages, one thing seems to have remained constant—human nature. The Israelites were only a little more than a month beyond the miracle of the parting of the Red Sea, which saved them from generations of slavery in Egypt, when they started grumbling about food. That's when God promised to give them manna, a daily supply of food from heaven. After a year of eating manna, however, the people started complaining again. "In Egypt we could eat all the fish we wanted, and there were cucumbers, melons, onions, and garlic. But we're starving out here, and the only food we have is this manna" (Numbers 11:5–6).

CHAPTER
4

ISAIAS · MOSES · DANIEL · DA VID · HII

The Bible is filled with wondrous tales of the heroic deeds of larger-than-life characters. Many of us know these stories well—so well that it's easy to gloss over their head-scratching details. Solomon was how rich? Jonah was swallowed by. . . a what? Yet that's where the magic lies in these stories.

SUPERHEROES OF THE FAITH

The famous observation architect Ludwig Mies van der Rohe made about his profession is also true of the Bible: "God is in the details."

For these stirring characters of the Bible, faith and strength were one and the same. Their legacies, and their mystique, live on.

Abraham is regarded as the founding figure of three of the world's major religions: Judaism, Christianity, and Islam. Since these faiths all look back to a single patriarch, they are sometimes called the "Abrahamic" religions. God chose Abraham as the man with whom he would create a special covenant.

ABRAHAM

DATE: 2166 BC TO 1991 BC   **GET THE WHOLE STORY:** READ GENESIS 11–25

It was because of this unique agreement that the Hebrews of the Old Testament considered themselves to be God's chosen people. The story of the Old Testament is essentially the story of the children of Abraham, the Jews, and of their special relationship with Abraham's God.

Like so many of the great stories of the Old Testament—and like stories and movies about superheroes in our time—the tale of Abraham is filled with wonders, miracles, and unearthly beings. The saga begins when God summons Abram (later Abraham), and tells him that he will be the founder of a great nation. Abram, however, is skeptical: How can he fulfill this vision when he and his wife Sarai (later Sarah) are not only childless, but also well into their 70s? God tells Abram that if he trusts in God's power, children will be forthcoming.

Abram trusts in God's promise; he and Sarai and Abram's nephew Lot and his family set out for Canaan, the land God had promised them. But first, Abraham heeds God's command and circumcises all of the males in his family. With their and Abraham's own circumcision, this practice becomes the "sign" of God's covenant with the Hebrew people. It remains a religious tradition practiced in Judaism to this day.

Ishmael and Isaac

Tradition has it that Abraham's ancestors were sellers of pagan idols. That story reminds us of perhaps Abraham's most significant contribution to world religion: he defied the social customs of his day by worshiping a single God rather than a pantheon of deities. After he leaves his home city of Haran, his commitment to his covenant with God takes him to Egypt, where he becomes wealthy—and where the old man not only fathers one child, but two. Convinced she will have no children, Sarah offers Abraham her young Egyptian slave Hagar to produce an heir. It works: The 86-year-old Abraham fathers a boy, Ishmael. Yet God had promised that Sarah would conceive, and in what must have seemed to be a miracle, she soon bears Abraham's second son, Isaac

Jealous of Hagar's and Ishmael's competing claims on her husband and his legacy, Sarah persuades Abraham to send them out into the desert. But God saves the duo and promises Hagar that Ishmael will sire a great nation through 12 sons—these are assumed by tradition to be the patriarchs of the 12 tribes of the Arabs. Yet God stipulates that the covenant will continue only through Isaac's line. Lot and his family, meanwhile, are caught up in the downfall of the cities of Sodom and Gomorrah, which are destroyed by God for their wickedness.

God Requests the Ultimate Sacrifice

Even as God declares Isaac's line will flourish, he demands another proof of Abraham's faith—one that appears to threaten the future of the chosen people. God tells Abraham he must offer up Isaac as a sacrifice, killing him as one might slaughter a young lamb. So great is Abraham's love and trust in God that he builds an altar, binds Isaac with rope and prepares to cut his throat. At the last moment, God sends an angel to stop Abraham, even as his hand is raised to kill his beloved son. Once again, Abraham's faith has been tested; once again God has shown the power of his love. Many students of the Bible see this early story of a father willingly sacrificing a son as a precursor of the central message of the New Testament: Jesus Christ is the Son of God, who willingly sacrifices himself to absolve men and women of their sins. As for Abraham, God rewards him, making Isaac and his descendants—as numerous as the stars—his chosen people.

A QUOTE FROM THE BIBLE
GENESIS 12:1–5

The LORD said to Abram:

Leave your country, your family, and your relatives and go to the land that I will show you. I will bless you and make your descendants into a great nation. You will become famous and be a blessing to others. I will bless anyone who blesses you, but I will put a curse on anyone who puts a curse on you. Everyone on earth will be blessed because of you. Abram was seventy-five years old when the LORD told him to leave the city of Haran. He obeyed and left with his wife Sarai, his nephew Lot, and all the possessions and slaves they had gotten while in Haran.

Stained glass window of Abraham and the sacrifice of Isaac.

"The LORD was with Joseph and made him successful in all that he did."

Genesis 39:23

ZAPHENATH-PANEAH

JOSEPH

DATE: 1914 BC TO 1805 BC   **GET THE WHOLE STORY:** READ GENESIS 30:22–24; GENESIS 37:1 TO GENESIS 50:26

Joseph, the elder son of Jacob and Rachel, is the founder of one of the great tribes of Israel. Charismatic, brilliant, and a diviner of dreams, he was marked for greatness: even after he was sold into slavery in Egypt, he started working as a household servant and ended up with authority over the entire estate. When he was falsely accused and jailed, the warden put him in charge of the whole prison. When freed from jail, he became the foremost advisor to the Pharaoh, Egypt's king.

It seemed to the ancient Egyptians that young scarab beetles emerged spontaneously from the burrow where they were born. Therefore they were worshiped as "Khepera," which means "he has come forth." This creative aspect of the scarab was associated with the creator god Atum.

Joseph was the Bill Gates of his day: a brilliant manager and business strategist, he seemed to share the gilded power of King Midas of Greek mythology: everything he touched turned to gold. His Hebrew name, in fact, means "The Lord increases." He was also blessed with the eerie capacity to predict the future by interpreting dreams. Joseph inspired others' confidence in him to such an unprecedented degree that when trouble threatened, Egypt's Pharaoh placed the fate of the entire country on the shoulders of this outsider—who was both non-Egyptian and an ex-convict—giving him full authority to handle a national crisis that could have devastated Egypt.

Escape Artist?

Joseph's life was a series of great escapes, a constant dance between frying pans and fires. As a young man, he was almost killed, but he miraculously survived—only to be sold into slavery in Egypt by his brothers, who resented the coat of many colors his father had made for him. Yet Joseph rose from slavery to a good position in Egypt. But his good fortune ended when his boss's wife began to flirt with him: workplace harassment, it seems, is as old as the Bible. Joseph ran away so fast that he left his coat in her hands—yet he still landed in prison. But even prison bars couldn't hold Joseph for long: he was released after two years, then embarked on an unprecedented rise to power. It was as if an unjustly accused prison inmate in our time received a presidential pardon—and then was appointed to be the penitent president's chief of staff.

Joseph's All-Access Pass

His ability to interpret dreams marked Joseph as a man of special power. In early civilizations, people thought dreaming opened the door to other worlds that couldn't be accessed any other way. When Joseph's fellow inmates—the king's assistant and chief cook—shared their dreams with him, his correct interpretations of them put him first in line to interpret the Pharaoh's dreams. Today researchers believe that dreams are either physiological or psychological phenomena. But Joseph's story, like others in the Bible, implies that dreams can connect us with worlds beyond our own—or even provide a sneak preview of the future.

A QUOTE FROM THE BIBLE
GENESIS 41:15–16

The king said to [Joseph], "I had a dream, yet no one can explain what it means. I am told that you can interpret dreams." "Your Majesty," Joseph answered, "I can't do it myself, but God can give a good meaning to your dreams."

Egyptian relief with a bull and an ankh, the symbol of life, from Luxor Temple, Thebes, Egypt

MOSES

DATE: 1526 BC TO 1406 BC   **GET THE WHOLE STORY:** READ EXODUS, NUMBERS, AND DEUTERONOMY

Moses was the first great leader of the Hebrew nation. He freed his people from slavery in Egypt and led them toward the land God had promised to their ancestor Abraham. His commanding presence and proximity to God made him a towering figure for his people, yet they did not always heed his words. Moses is credited as the writer of most of the first five books of the Bible, which Jews call the Law or the Torah; they are the sacred foundation of Judaism. Moses' life story is filled with miracles and marvels, but it also offers memorable depictions of the sad failings of human nature.

Moses was actually a Hebrew descendant of the people who immigrated to Egypt from Canaan. His ancestors, Jacob and his twelve sons, came to Egypt to survive a famine (Genesis 42–50). In the four centuries that followed their arrival, the family grew into a nation—but sadly, they were still a nation of Egyptian slaves. At the time of Moses' birth, the Pharaoh of Egypt had ordered the killing of male Hebrew babies as a brutal means of controlling the Israelites' population, for he wanted to keep them from becoming strong enough to fight for their freedom. It was during this period that Moses was born, and the Pharaoh's grim edict provided the backdrop for his first great escape.

Baby in a Basket

Moses escaped Pharaoh's order to kill Hebrew baby boys because his mother hid him in a basket at the edge of the Nile River. In a great twist of providence, he was found and rescued—and his benefactor was an Egyptian princess who adopted him into the royal family. Thus Moses enjoyed the privileges of royalty and learned the protocols of Egypt's court, knowledge that served him well when he later faced the Pharaoh as a petitioner for his people (Exodus 1–2).

An Exile

From his infancy, Moses was thus intricately tied to two different worlds. He was raised as a child of royalty, yet was taken care of by a Hebrew nurse—who just happened to be his own mother! Since the Hebrews were oppressed by the Egyptian government, his loyalties were divided. When Moses witnessed an Egyptian beating a Hebrew, he cast his lot with the people of his birth: he killed the Egyptian—and he thought he had gotten away with it. The next day, though, he realized that his true identity was no longer a secret.

The Pharaoh set out to kill Moses, but once again the wily young man escaped. Leaving behind everything he knew, Moses fled to the desert, where he became a shepherd, married, and had children. It seemed he had made a clean getaway and established a new life. Then he came upon a bush that seemed to be burning—though it never burned up—and heard the voice of God. (Read Exodus 2–3.) Here was a call he could not escape: Moses had met his destiny.

A QUOTE FROM THE BIBLE
EXODUS 8:20–25

The LORD said to Moses:

Early tomorrow morning, while the king is on his way to the river, go and say to him, "The LORD commands you to let his people go, so they can worship him. If you don't, he will send swarms of flies to attack you, your officials, and every citizen of your country. Houses will be full of flies, and the ground will crawl with them.

"The LORD's people in Goshen won't be bothered by flies, but your people in the rest of the country will be tormented by them. That's how you will know that the LORD is here in Egypt. This miracle will happen tomorrow."

The LORD kept his promise—the palace and the homes of the royal officials swarmed with flies, and the rest of the country was infested with them as well. Then the king sent for Moses and Aaron and told them, "Go sacrifice to your God, but stay here in Egypt."

SAMSON

DATE: 1100 BC TO 1055 BC   **GET THE WHOLE STORY:** READ JUDGES 13:1 TO JUDGES 16:31

Many heroes of the Bible demonstrate strength of will, strength of character, or strength of faith. But Samson's power was not a matter of metaphor; he was truly an Old Testament muscle man. No steroids for him! Before he was born, Samson's parents were visited by an angel. His mother, who had previously been unable to bear children, was given strict instructions for raising her son: no wine or other spirits—and no haircuts!

Following these rules was part of the Nazirite Vow, which is a commitment to an ancient holy lifestyle described in the book of Numbers. Several other Bible superheroes, including the prophet Samuel and possibly even the apostle Paul of the New Testament, were Nazirites.

Man's Strength . . . and Weakness

Certainly, a vow of this kind of abstinence would strengthen a warrior's spirit, but Samson believed his superhuman strength was associated not only with the vow, but also with his long hair. And what strength it was! He once tore a lion in half; another time he killed 1,000 Philistines using, of all things, the jawbone of a donkey. Samson was once in a city called Gaza where some men were planning to kill him at dawn. He left the city carrying with him the city gates—doors, posts, bars and all—still locked. Talk about power lifting!

Samson fell in love with a woman named Delilah, a temptress from the Sorek Valley. The Philistine rulers bargained with Delilah to discover Samson's source of strength, so Delilah made it a game with Samson, teasing him into giving her the reason for his strength.

Three times Samson gave her bogus answers—tie me up with seven bowstrings, use new ropes, weave my hair on a loom—but each time he used his strength to free himself.

Delilah continued to pester Samson until he finally told her the truth:

I have belonged to God ever since I was born, so my hair has never been cut. If it were ever cut off, my strength would leave me, and I would be as weak as anyone else (Judges 16:17).

Delilah squealed, and while Samson was sleeping, the Philistine rulers cut off his seven braids. When the strong man awoke, his strength was gone.

The Philistines grabbed Samson and poked out his eyes. They took him to the prison in Gaza and chained him up. Then they put him to work, turning a millstone to grind grain (Judges 16:21).

But the Philistines didn't cut his hair any more, so it started growing back—and so did his strength. Eventually, Samson gambled away his leadership and his influence, but even in death, he brought scores of Philistines to justice. Whatever his human faults, he stands out as one of the Bible's superheroes.

Faithful Men

The writer of the book of Hebrews included Samson in his list of faithful men and women of the Old Testament: *What else can I say? There isn't enough time to tell about Gideon, Barak, Samson, Jephthah, David, Samuel, and the prophets. Their faith helped them conquer kingdoms, and because they did right, God made promises to them. They closed the jaws of lions and put out raging fires and escaped from the swords of their enemies. Although they were weak, they were given the strength and power to chase foreign armies away* (Hebrews 11:32–34).

A QUOTE FROM THE BIBLE
JUDGES 16:15-17

"Samson," Delilah said, "you claim to love me, but you don't mean it! You've made me look like a fool three times now, and you still haven't told me why you are so strong."

Delilah started nagging and pestering him day after day, until he couldn't stand it any longer.

Finally, Samson told her the truth. "I have belonged to God ever since I was born, so my hair has never been cut. If it were ever cut off, my strength would leave me, and I would be as weak as anyone else."

What made Solomon, King David's son and heir, so wise? According to the Bible, at the outset of Solomon's reign, God allowed him to ask for any gift he desired—and Solomon surprised him, requesting not wealth but wisdom. Because God was pleased with his request, God granted Solomon not only wisdom, but also riches, power, respect, and influence.

SOLOMON

DATE: 1000 BC TO 930 BC   **GET THE WHOLE STORY:** READ 1 KINGS 1–11 AND 2 CHRONICLES 1–9

One of Solomon's most famous judgments involved returning a baby to his mother. Two women claimed the child was hers. When Solomon ordered that the baby be cut in two and half the child be awarded to each of them, the real mother cried out. The other (who was accused of accidentally killing her own son, then switching the babies) was willing to let the child die. Solomon's ploy revealed the truth.

A Visitor from the East

The Queen of Sheba, a land in southwestern Arabia that maintained a trade alliance with Israel, traveled to Solomon's palace to see for herself if his reputation as the wisest man in the world was deserved. According to the Bible, she went to Jerusalem, the capital city, to test Solomon with the most difficult questions, and *"he answered every question, no matter how difficult it was."*

The Queen was amazed at Solomon's wisdom. She was breathless when she saw his palace, the food on his table, his officials, all his servants in their uniforms; and the sacrifices he offered at the LORD's temple.

She said: Solomon, in my own country I had heard about your wisdom and all you've done. But I didn't believe it until I saw it with my own eyes! And there's so much I didn't hear about. You are greater than I was told. (2 Chronicles 9:2–6)

Solomon's Wisdom: Absent Without Leave

Solomon appears to have been wiser in his youth than as a grown man. The wisdom God had granted him developed into great financial and diplomatic success. But as they so often do in this world, his growing wealth and power revealed fault lines in his character, and his follies began to match his riches.

At the height of his kingdom, Solomon had 700 wives and 300 concubines, many from other countries. In that day and time, polygamy was not uncommon, but it was not the rule among the Hebrews. Their law encouraged monogamy—marriage between one man and one woman. Besotted with his enormous harem, Solomon let his many wives lull him into foreign forms of worship. According to his own story, Solomon's wisdom had come from his faithful union with God. By the end of his reign, though, he loved his wives and riches more than he loved God.

Solomon's book of Proverbs extols the positive values of a God-centered life, but his later writings in the book of Ecclesiastes—written in the voice of experience—lament the futility of life lived in pursuit of everything except God. In his disillusionment, Solomon seemed to come full circle: "Respect and obey God! This is what life is all about." (Ecclesiastes 12:13)

If the real test of a nation's leader is the legacy he leaves behind, Solomon failed. Exhausted from the amount of work it took to support Solomon's extravagant ways, his people lost their faith in their leaders. After Solomon died, his kingdom was split in two: for all his early wisdom and later riches, he left behind an Israel whose house was divided.

A QUOTE FROM THE BIBLE
1 KINGS 4:30–34

[Solomon] was wiser than anyone else in the world, including the wisest people of the east and of Egypt.... Solomon became famous in every country around Judah and Israel. Solomon wrote three thousand wise sayings and composed more than one thousand songs. He could talk about all kinds of plants, from large trees to small bushes, and he taught about animals, birds, reptiles, and fish. Kings all over the world heard about Solomon's wisdom and sent people to listen to him teach.

"Wisdom is worth more than silver; it makes you much richer than gold."

Proverbs 3:14

THE MYSTERIES OF SOLOMON'S TEMPLE

A QUOTE FROM THE BIBLE

1 KINGS 6:11–14

The LORD told Solomon:

If you obey my commands and do what I say, I will keep the promise I made to your father David. I will live among my people Israel in this temple you are building, and I will not desert them.

So Solomon's workers finished building the temple.

BRONZE ALTAR

Families gathered outdoors as priests sacrificed lambs, goats, bulls, and doves. Their collected blood would carry away the sin of the penitent, prayerful people. Blood was sprinkled daily upon the horns and base of the altar, then onto the barrier tapestry ("veil") inside the temple. Animal remains were eaten

THE SEA

The sea held 17,500 gallons of water, used for ceremonial washing.

ART

Solomon carved angelic beings (cherubim) and palm trees on the walls of the temple and overlaid its entire interior with gold. The Bible says that the temple was decorated with various colors and inlaid with turquoise and marble.

THE HOLY PLACE

Only priests could enter this most sacred interior, which was about 90 feet long and 30 feet wide. The ceiling soared some 4 1/2 stories above the floor. Complete biblical descriptions can be found in 1 Kings 5–8, 1 Chronicles 28, 29 and 2 Chronicles 2–5.

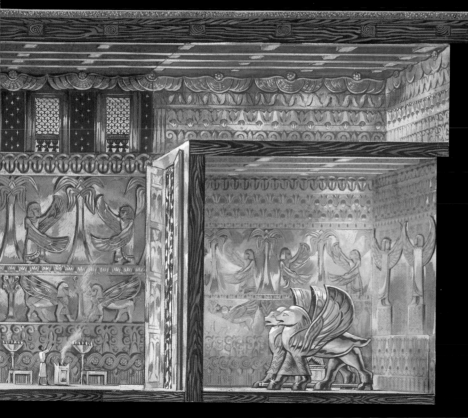

The temple is shown here with the north wall removed. East is at the left; west is to the right. Notice the shaft of morning sunlight as it hits the solid gold floor and walls, filling the interior with golden light.

Hugh Claycombe

In Old Testament times, societies were strictly divided along gender lines: a woman's place was generally considered to be within the home, while men hunted, farmed, fished, tended sheep, and filled most other occupations. Yet a number of strong female figures join men like Abraham, Joseph, Moses, and Samson as heroes of biblical tales.

ESTHER

DATE: CA. 400 BC   **GET THE WHOLE STORY:** READ ESTHER 1–10

The story of the courage of Ruth and her mother-in-law, Naomi, is told in the book of Ruth, while the tale of Judith—the daring warrior who beheads the invading Assyrian general, Holofernes—is told in the book of Judith, one of the books that is included in Roman Catholic and Orthodox Bibles, but not most Protestant Bibles. One of the most stirring tales is that of Esther, who saved all the Jews living in the Persian Empire from certain slaughter. Her story is told in the book of Esther.

From Orphan to Queen to Savior

Esther, who was originally named Hadassah, was orphaned at an early age and adopted by her cousin Mordecai, a Jew who occupied a high position at the court of Xerxes, the king of Persia (modern-day Iran and Iraq), at a time when there were many Jews living in that nation. Hadassah was beautiful, lively, and intelligent; she caught the eye of the king, who did not know she was a Jew. When they married, she changed her name to Esther. Some time after the marriage, Mordecai learned that two of the king's advisors were conspiring to murder him; he told Esther, who alerted Xerxes, saving his life—and earning further royal favor for both Mordecai and Esther.

Xerxes' chief minister, Haman, grew jealous of Mordecai's increasing influence, and he concocted a plan to massacre Mordecai, Esther, and all the Jews then living in Persia in a single day. But after Esther and Mordecai learned of the scheme, Esther outwitted Haman and convinced Xerxes of Haman's wickedness. In the end, Haman was hanged upon the very gallows he had ordered built for the execution of Mordecai. All the Jews of Persia were saved, and some 75,000 of Haman's troops and followers across the land were put to death. The Jews then celebrated their deliverance with a triumphant celebration, called Purim, which is a Babylonian term for the lots that Haman used to determine on which day the attack against the Jews was to take place.

Esther's Feast: Purim

Thousands of years after Esther's story was first told, the feast of Purim remains one of the most joyous annual events on the Jewish calendar. Readings from the book of Esther are a highlight of Purim, with the villain Haman often being loudly booed by the congregation in the synagogue, while the heroic Esther and Mordecai are cheered. The feast often features an exchange of gifts; the playing of harmless pranks; and parades with masked characters dressed as Haman, Esther, and others from the story. With its tale of survival in an alien land, the book of Esther reminds Jews of their long history of wandering and of the times when they were delivered from evil by God's hand, as in the story of Moses and the first Passover. The largest modern American Jewish women's service organization, Hadassah, takes its name from Esther's original Hebrew name.

A QUOTE FROM THE BIBLE
ESTHER 5:1–5

Three days later, Esther dressed in her royal robes and went to the inner court of the palace in front of the throne. The king was sitting there, facing the open doorway. He was happy to see Esther, and he held out the gold scepter to her.

When Esther came up and touched the tip of the scepter, the king said, "Esther, what brings you here? Just ask, and I will give you as much as half of my kingdom."

Esther answered, "Your Majesty, please come with Haman to a dinner I will prepare for you later today."

The king said to his servants, "Hurry and get Haman, so we can accept Esther's invitation."

Francesco Fontebasso (1709–1769)
Esther and Ahasuerus (Xerxes)
Parish Church, Povo, Italy

DANIEL

DATE: 620 BC TO 540 BC   **GET THE WHOLE STORY:** READ THE BOOK OF DANIEL

Most superheroes of the Bible are distinguished by their mighty deeds, but in one case Daniel stood out for what he *didn't* do: feed himself! According to the biblical account, after he was imprisoned and lived for ten days on nothing but vegetables and water, Daniel and his three Hebrew companions looked far healthier than their peers, who dined on food fit for a king. After three years of this regimen, Daniel and his friends were not only declared superior to other people—they were handpicked to serve the king. (Read Daniel 1.)

Like so many other heroes of the Bible, Daniel found himself a captive when his astonishing deeds began. As was the custom of the day, when the Babylonians conquered Judah, the best and brightest Jews were taken back and assimilated into Babylon. This policy advanced Babylon's strength, and also assured that Judah's best warriors weren't left behind in the homeland to lead a revolt.

Daniel came as a captive, but refused to be assimilated into the spiritual culture of his captors, even as he acquired political power and respect. He continued to follow the dietary restrictions that God had placed upon his people, the Jews, and he continued to worship in the way he was taught as a child. This faithfulness was not just a sacrifice for him and his friends: it landed him in hot water—and his friends in a hot furnace. Daniel was thrown into a lion's den for praying to God. His friends were thrown into a fiery oven for refusing to worship idols. Their faith set them apart and threatened their lives, but it also provided an avenue for God to honor them—and thus reveal himself—in the kingdom of Babylon. (Read Daniel 1–4.)

Daniel's Friends and the Fiery Furnace

Daniel's friends were thrown into a furnace that was probably used for smelting ore. The charge against them was bogus—but the heat was real. How did they survive?

Was the escape from the fiery furnace any more spectacular than a firewalker's stunt? Ordinary people have shown they can scurry across hot coals without getting burned. Actually, though, firewalkers move quickly over ash-coated coals that have cooled down below 500° F. Daniel's friends strolled leisurely in a furnace blazing at nearly 2000° F—hot enough to kill the soldiers who threw them into it. Yet they survived. (Read Daniel 3.)

Daniel's Escape from the Hungry Lions

When lions aren't hungry, they are content to lie basking in the sun for up to twenty hours a day. A man might survive in a den of lions whose stomachs were full. But in a den of hungry lions, odds are he wouldn't last an hour. What chance would he have against beasts that stand nearly fifty inches high, weigh more than 400 pounds, have razor-like claws and two-inch teeth? These sinewy predators can take down a 900-pound zebra!

So when Daniel was placed in a lion's den as his punishment for not praying to the king's gods, how did he survive? He couldn't leave the pit, because it was sealed with a stone. He had nothing with which to keep the lions at bay—no whip, no chair. Could the lions have just been fed? Evidently not—for after Daniel was released from the den, the men who had accused him of wrongdoing were thrown into it, and the lions attacked them all immediately. (Read Daniel 6.)

Daniel's story also appears in two Apocryphal books: *Susanna* and *Bel and the Dragon.*

A QUOTE FROM THE BIBLE
DANIEL 6:19–23

At daybreak the king got up and ran to the pit. He was anxious and shouted, "Daniel, you were faithful and served your God. Was he able to save you from the lions?"

Daniel answered, "Your Majesty, I hope you live forever! My God knew that I was innocent, and he sent an angel to keep the lions from eating me. Your Majesty, I have never done anything to hurt you."

The king was relieved to hear Daniel's voice, and he gave orders for him to be taken out of the pit. Daniel's faith in his God had kept him from being harmed.

Blast furnace

Daniel in the lion's den

It's a whale of a tale: When God called upon Jonah, a holy man, to preach to the people who lived in an enemy city, Jonah was afraid. Rather than obey God's call, he ran away. But as the great boxer Joe Louis once said of an intimidated opponent, "He can run, but he can't hide." And Jonah couldn't hide from God: when he tried to make his getaway, the LORD arranged special accommodations for his reluctant prophet—inside the belly of a whale.

JONAH

DATE: CA. 760 BC   **GET THE WHOLE STORY:** READ THE BOOK OF JONAH

After God called Jonah to preach to the people of Nineveh, he jumped into a boat going the other direction. Suddenly a great storm arose on the sea—a clear reminder to Jonah of God's displeasure. (Read Jonah 1:4–16.) What kind of storm did God send to afflict Jonah?

Stormy Weather

Hurricanes are most closely associated with tropical waters, such as the Caribbean Sea and the Gulf of Mexico. However, hurricane-like storms are not unheard of in the Mediterranean Sea. In 1947, 1969, 1982, 1983, and 1995, intense storms resembling hurricanes swept across this normally placid sea. Lack of data makes it difficult to classify these storms, but some scientists have labeled them "polar lows." In satellite pictures, they appear very similar to hurricanes. They develop rapidly, grow to hundreds of miles in diameter, and carry winds of gale force or stronger. A German weather ship passing through the 1995 storm two days before it peaked reported sustained winds of 84 mph.

A storm of this type would produce hazardous conditions at sea, with very high waves, driving spray, and low visibility. It's no wonder the sailors on Jonah's boat were so frightened. But what caused such a powerful storm—one that would normally rage on for days—to suddenly subside the moment the seamen threw Jonah overboard?

Nineveh: Behind Enemy Lines

When Jonah felt God's call to preach to Nineveh, he first sought refuge by heading in the opposite direction. His hesitation is understandable: Why preach good news to your most dangerous enemies—particularly when such helpful warnings might only make them a stronger nation?

Nineveh—one of the world's most ancient cities—was located on the Tigris River in northern Iraq, across from modern-day Mosul. It was the capital of the Assyrian Empire, a world superpower poised to engulf Israel, Jonah's homeland. Yet after his initial reluctance, this notable patriot traveled through enemy territory to warn his own foes of their impending doom.

"Then they threw Jonah overboard, and the sea calmed down."

Jonah 1:15

unnatural
disasters

CHAPTER 5

Many ancient cultures interpreted deadly natural disasters, extremes of weather and events in the heavens as messages, or portents, from God, or as divine punishments for humanity's misdeeds. There are several biblical accounts of God-sent natural disasters, as well as some that are unnatural: they defy explanation even by modern science.

Not every clap of thunder can be interpreted as God's voice of judgment, but in the case of the following unnatural disasters, the Bible certainly depicts God's hand at work in the world. Whether the misdeeds that caused such divine retribution took place in the privacy of the temple or the public streets of the city, the Bible makes clear that God was justly punishing those who ignored his laws.

PSALM 9:6-8

Our enemies are destroyed completely
for all time. Their cities are torn down,
and they will never be remembered
again. You rule forever, LORD,
and you are on your throne, ready for
judgment. You judge the world fairly
and treat all nations with justice.

In its first book, Genesis, the Bible describes a devastating flood, sent by God, that covered the entire surface of the earth, destroying all life except that of Noah, his family, and the animals Noah had secured in an oddly-shaped boat. Some believe the story describes a flood that covered not the entire globe, but only the portion of it known to the ancients. Which was it?

the flood

Nearly every culture on Earth tells a primal tale of a cataclysmic flood that afflicted its ancestors in the distant past. Among the most famous are the story of Noah's Flood in Genesis and the "Epic of Gilgamesh," another account of a great deluge, written in Babylonian cuneiform. It's interesting to note that a great many of these ancient stories share two curious details: 1) The flood was worldwide; and 2) A few fortunate people survived in a boat.

However, if the entire planet was once covered by a flood, as the Bible and other stories state, a simple question arises—where did those vast quantities of water come from?

Genesis 7:11 describes two sources: "the fountains of the great deep" and the "windows of heaven." Subterranean lakes exist today beneath Greece, Brazil, Iraq, North America, and elsewhere—and then there are the hot underground reservoirs of water that supply Old Faithful and other geysers in Yellowstone National Park. Could the "fountains of the deep" have been similar subterranean chambers in ancient times? Or perhaps they were tsunamis unleashed by gigantic tectonic forces, like the mammoth Indian Ocean waves that killed more than 225,000 people in 2004.

The term "windows of heaven" is less easily defined. Many say it might refer to a vapor canopy that surrounded Earth—similar to the ozone layer—providing additional protection against radiation and creating a tropical climate on the planet's surface. Such a heat-trapping envelope around the globe might explain the lush plant material found preserved in Antarctic ice.

Another theory posits that the water came from the heavens in the form of icy meteors. Consider this interesting evidence:

- Geologists have identified more than 150 major meteoric impact sites on our planet. Some scientists estimate as many as 3 million meteors may have hit the planet over the ages.
- The Moon, our closest neighbor, bears more than 300,000 impact craters.
- The asteroid belt between Mars and Jupiter hints that a planet once existing there was destroyed in an explosion.

If Earth did indeed experience a divinely-appointed rendezvous with a meteor, it could have triggered a deadly chain reaction, breaking the planet's crust and releasing geysers of waters from the deep. Massive earthquakes and volcanic eruptions around the world would have thrown thousands of tons of ash and sulfur particulates into the atmosphere, generating an immense downpour of rain from the "heavens" and shutting out the light of the Sun, killing vegetation.

No matter how the flood started or ended, our planet bears significant evidence that such cataclysmic astronomical events have occurred in the past. The signs include worldwide silt deposits and layered strata; huge coal beds composed of swiftly buried plant and animal material; masses of tangled skeletal animal remains; oceanic fossils on mountaintops; and immense water erosion from draining floodwaters. Scientists now believe just such a meteor impact 65 million years ago put an end to the long reign of the dinosaurs. To learn more about the Bible's big flood, read Genesis 6–8.

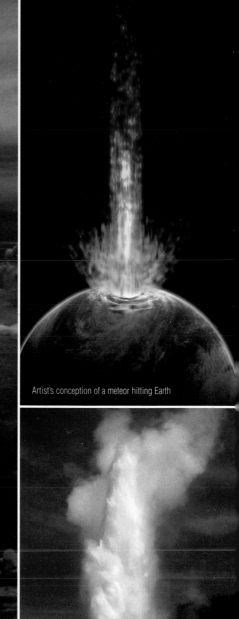

Artist's conception of a meteor hitting Earth

Old Faithful in Yellowstone National Park

fascinating facts related

- Many of the ancient flood stories include a leader with a name strangely similar to the one used in the Bible's account—Noah. Among them are: Noh, Nu, Nau, Nuh, Manu ("ma" means water, "nu" means Noah), Manoa ("Noah's waters"), Minne (Sioux for "water"), and more.

- The Chinese word for "boat" is a combination of three ancient symbols: "vessel," "eight," and "mouth," which together tell the story of eight people saved by a boat.

- The Timaeus of Plato, written c. 360 BC, refers to the "great deluge of all."

- The Epic of Gilgamesh describes the Akkadian collapse in which "many stars were falling from the sky." The "Curse of Akkad," dated to about 2200 BC, speaks of "flaming potsherds raining from the sky." Could this text refer to a meteor shower?

- The summit of Mount Everest is composed of deep-marine limestone, with fossils of ocean-bottom dwelling crinoids—at 29,035 feet above sea level.

Chronology of the Flood as recounted in Genesis 7, 8

40 days
"The sky opened like windows, and rain poured down for forty days and nights." (Genesis 7:11-12)

After 150 more days
Waters covered the earth before it began to recede. (7:24)

After 114 more days
The water began to recede and Noah sent out a raven from the ark. (8:6-7)

After 7 more days
Noah released a dove for the first time. However, "Deep water was still everywhere, and the dove could not find a place to land. So it flew back to the boat. Noah held out his hand and helped it back in." (8:9)

to the flood

- Whale skeletons have been found at 440 feet above sea level north of Lake Ontario, 500 feet above sea level in Vermont, and 600 feet above sea level in the Montreal-Quebec area.

- Tectonic upheaval could shift mountains and drop the ocean floor, forming the enormous basins for the floodwaters' runoff and creating the deep oceans we see today, which cover 70 percent of the earth.

- In 2003, Ohio State University scientists drilled ice cores in the Peruvian Andes that indicate a global climate change may have occurred approximately 5,000 years ago.

- Geologists studying the deadly eruption of Mount St. Helens in Washington State on May 18, 1980, were amazed at how quickly powerful lava flows carved through solid rock and laid down hundreds of feet of new rock. In a matter of hours, rather than millions of years, the massive eruption created a canyon some $1/40^{th}$ the scale of the Grand Canyon in Arizona.

- Volcanic ash from Mount St. Helens spewed into the atmosphere and changed weather patterns around the world for years after its violent eruption. Many volcanoes erupting at the same time would have been catastrophic, changing Earth's climate and perhaps ushering in a new Ice Age.

Image: Mt. St. Helens, WA, USA.

After 7 more days
Noah released the dove a second time, and this time it returned with a green leaf in its beak. (8:10-11)

After 7 more days
Noah released the dove a third time. The bird did not return. (8:12)

After 50 more days
Noah and his family waited for the ground to dry completely before they stepped off the ark. (8:13-14)

Total: 375 days
One year and ten days passed from the day the flood started until Noah and his family left the ark.

sodom and gomorrah

Located along the salty flats near the Dead Sea, the two cities of Sodom and Gomorrah were notorious in biblical times for the extravagant misdeeds of their inhabitants. Today, the cities' names are synonymous with iniquity and debauchery; our word sodomy is a modern echo of Sodom's depravity.

According to the Bible, Abraham, the great ancestor of the Israelites and other Semitic tribes, was disturbed when he learned that God intended to destroy Sodom and Gomorrah, where his nephew Lot lived. Abraham negotiated with God, asking him to spare the cities if ten righteous people could be found living in them. God agreed, but the census of the righteous did not even reach two digits. Lot, having been warned, fled with his wife and two unmarried daughters. His wife looked back and was destroyed; only Lot and his daughters escaped death (Genesis 19).

Remnants Found

The Bible indicates that not only Sodom and Gomorrah, but three other "cities of the plain" were destroyed as well on that fateful day. In the 1960s and 1970s, an expedition originally headed by noted biblical archaeologist Paul W. Lapp discovered what is believed to be the location of the destroyed cities. The area, located south of the Dead Sea, contains asphalt, sulfur (brimstone), petroleum, tar pits, and natural gas.

Archaeologist Bryant Wood suggests that "these combustible materials could have been forced from the earth by subterranean pressure brought about by an earthquake resulting from the shifting of the bounding faults. If these combustibles were ignited by lightning or some other agency as they came spewing forth from the ground, it would indeed result in a holocaust such as described in Genesis 19."

Excavations of the sites have revealed large amounts of ash along with evidence of scorching. Others even appear to have yielded remnants of balls of burnt sulfur.

Perhaps the fate that befell "the cities of the plain" was a natural disaster; it may have been the deeds of their inhabitants, inspiring God's wrath, that were unnatural.

A QUOTE FROM THE BIBLE
GENESIS 19:27–29

That same morning Abraham got up and went to the place where he had stood and spoken with the LORD. He looked down toward Sodom and Gomorrah and saw smoke rising from all over the land—it was like a flaming furnace.

When God destroyed the cities of the valley where Lot lived, he remembered his promise to Abraham and saved Lot from the terrible destruction.

The Dead Sea, Israel

one **salty** wife

What makes the Dead Sea dead? Salt. Lots of it! Or should we say . . . Lot's of it? As the book of Genesis tells the story, two angels warned Lot of the coming destruction of Sodom and Gomorrah. Taking Lot, his wife, and their two daughters by their hands, the angels led the family of four out of the city. Once beyond the city gates, one of the angels said, "Run for your lives! Don't even look back" (Genesis 19:17). The family fled, but Lot's wife, perhaps momentarily regretting the loss of her home and belongings, defied the angelic injunction, looked behind her, and was instantly turned into a pillar of salt (Genesis 19:26).

The mountains of salt that nudge up against the Dead Sea have long been a source of wealth for the kingdoms that controlled them and thus a catalyst for ongoing conflict. Since salt erodes easily, wind and weather act as constant sculptors of the land here, forming it into pinnacles and pillars. One particular crag near the south end of the Dead Sea is called "Bint Sheik Lot," or "Lot's Wife," since it is said to resemble the shape of a woman.

A Divine Name-Check

Jesus actually mentioned Lot's wife when speaking to his disciples about the end of the world. He urged his followers to "remember what happened to Lot's wife. People who try to save their lives will lose them, and those who lose their lives will save them" (Luke 17:32–33).

top ten ways to

1   2   3   4   5

Moses rose to prominence as a leader when he confronted Egypt's Pharaoh with one of history's great exhortations: "Let my people go!" Living as captives under brutal taskmasters, Moses' people, the Hebrews, had become a nation of oppressed slaves. Pharaoh listened to Moses' plea, but refused it. In response, Moses warned that God would send a series of plagues (disasters) upon the land if the Hebrews weren't released. Again Pharaoh refused, and God made good on the threat.

fight a pharaoh

6   7   8   9   10

Ten plagues swept through Egypt, one at a time (Exodus 7:14–12:30).

PLAGUE NO.1
All the waters of Egypt—rivers, lakes, canals, and reservoirs—were turned to blood. Even the water stored in jars ran sanguine with blood.

PLAGUE NO.2
Frogs emerged everywhere, pried into everything, then died, leaving a decaying, slimy mess.

PLAGUE NO.3
Every speck of dust in Egypt was transformed into a nasty gnat, getting into the Egyptians' mouths, noses, ears, and eyes.

PLAGUE NO.4
Thick, undulating swarms of dirty, pestilential flies covered the land and filled the houses, breeding hosts of maggots.

PLAGUE NO.5
Every livestock animal belonging to the Egyptians died, while those belonging to the Hebrews were unaffected. This plague was especially bitter since the Egyptians were an agrarian culture; they depended on oxen to pull their wagons, horses for transportation and defense, and cattle for food.

PLAGUE NO.6
Festering boils and open sores suddenly broke out all over the bodies of the Egyptian people and their pets.

PLAGUE NO.7
Hail rained from the sky and lightning struck the earth, destroying crops and stripping the bark from trees. The area where the Hebrews lived, however, was untouched.

PLAGUE NO.8
Massive swarms of locusts descended on what remained of the hail-damaged crops. The Bible says nothing green remained in Egypt after the locusts devoured the land.

PLAGUE NO.9
Moses stretched out his hand, and darkness fell upon the land. The unnatural gloom lasted for three days, blinding the Egyptians. Yet, miraculously, the Hebrews could see.

PLAGUE NO.10
In the tenth and last plague, God sent the Angel of Death to kill all the firstborn children of the hard-hearted Egyptians. God told the Hebrew people how to ensure the Angel of Death would "pass over" the homes of God's faithful people—they were to mark their doorposts with the blood of sheep or goats. In the end, all Hebrew children were saved, while all Egyptian firstborn children died—including the Pharaoh's. This was the first Passover.

A QUOTE FROM THE BIBLE
EXODUS 12:31

During the night the king sent for Moses and Aaron and told them, "Get your people out of my country and leave us alone! Go and worship the LORD, as you have asked."

Snakes on a Plain

Even before the plagues, Moses and his brother Aaron manifested God's power to pharaoh through amazing signs. Following God's instruction, Aaron threw down his wooden staff, and it became a snake. Pharaoh called upon his magicians to duplicate the feat. Amazingly the sorcerers did so, only to watch, helpless, as the snake from Aaron's staff quickly ate the pharaoh's snakes (Read Exodus 7:8–13.)

earth quakes

Throughout the Bible, earthquakes were a tangible, rumbling punctuation of significant events. Sometimes they were perceived as a form of judgment, sometimes as a form of emphasis, but never could they be ignored.

Mt. Sinai Rocks and Rolls

Mt. Sinai is hallowed, for here God gave Moses the Ten Commandments, in a true multimedia experience that included smoke, lightning, thunder, and the shaking of the earth. The Bible says this quake was intended to emphasize the significance of the Law the Hebrews were about to receive and the presence of the one from whom they would receive it (Exodus 19).

Rebel with a Lost Cause

Jewish history recounts the forty years the Hebrews wandered through the wilderness between Egypt and Canaan. During their time in the desert, some of the men began to doubt Moses' leadership. Korah was such a man. The Bible records his rebellion, and God's response: The earth quaked, and the ground swallowed those who followed Korah in his mutiny (Numbers 16).

Jonathan's Victory

Jonathan was the son of King Saul (Israel's first king) and a soldier in the king's army. In this military capacity, Jonathan confronted an enemy outpost without his father's knowledge, but with faith that God would give him a victory. Although he was an excellent warrior, Jonathan's victory was actually secured only when an earthquake panicked his enemies, the Philistines, causing them to run "in every direction like melted wax" (1 Samuel 14).

Elijah's Rendezvous with God

The life of an Old Testament prophet was physically and emotionally draining. After Elijah fought one of his most famous battles, he was utterly depleted—whipped! To renew his energy, God told Elijah to go to the side of a mountain and wait to see God pass. Elijah held on, clutching a tree or rock, as the wind ripped, the earth quaked, and fire blazed. Then, appearing on a gentle breeze, God met with Elijah and renewed his spirit (1 Kings 19).

The Crucifixion

One of the most gripping scenes in Mel Gibson's movie *The Passion of the Christ* is at the moment of Jesus' death. The camera angle is from the sky looking down, and the movie screen itself seems to undulate slightly. The Bible states that an earthquake occurred just as Jesus drew his last breath—a quake so powerful that "rocks split apart" and "graves opened" (Matthew 27:51–52).

Paul and Silas in Prison

New Testament prisons were, in most cases, dark, damp dungeons. There were no benches to sit on and every prisoner was shackled to the wall. That was the grim situation Paul and Silas once found themselves in. Brutally beaten and imprisoned, they sat on the floor with their feet chained to heavy blocks of wood. Even so, they were praying and singing in defiance of their captors and in celebration of their Lord. As they sang, an earthquake shook the foundation of the prison, its doors flew open, and their chains fell off. Free at last!—by the hand of God (Acts 16:16–34).

A QUOTE FROM THE BIBLE
HEBREWS 12:25–28

Make sure that you obey the one who speaks to you. The people did not escape, when they refused to obey the one who spoke to them at Mount Sinai. Do you think you can possibly escape, if you refuse to obey the one who speaks to you from heaven? When God spoke the first time, his voice shook only the earth. This time he has promised to shake the earth once again, and heaven too.

The words "once again" mean that these created things will someday be shaken and removed. Then what cannot be shaken will last. We should be grateful that we were given a kingdom that cannot be shaken. And in this kingdom we please God by worshiping him and by showing him great honor and respect.

CHAPTER

6

ANGELS and
DEMONS

HEBREWS 13:2

Be sure to welcome strangers into your home. By doing this, some people have welcomed angels as guests, without even knowing it.

From the Garden of Eden in Genesis to the end-of-the-world prophecies in Revelation, angels play a significant biblical role as God's servants and messengers. Nor were these heavenly beings ethereal or illusory: men and women observed angels, walked with angels, talked with angels. Though the unexpected appearance of an angel must have been startling, the tidings they brought were often of great joy.

Two angels are identified by name several times in the Bible—Michael and Gabriel. Other important Jewish writings of the time that the early Christians would have known about also identify the angels Raphael, Jeremiel, and Uriel. Many translations of the Bible also mention cherubim and seraphim as well as other terms, suggesting that God's heavenly host is composed of many different groups.

Angel-themed gifts and collectibles are hot items these days; they are pleasant reminders that there is a world beyond our own. But to really grasp the concept of citizens from another dimension moving among us as we work and play challenges our grasp of the possible. Reading about the angels who weave in and out of people's lives in the Bible makes us wonder if these supernatural beings weave in and out of our own lives, suffusing our passage through this world with whispering wings of grace.

ANGELS
in the **old** testament

Throughout the Old Testament, angels intervened in earthly life to perform a variety of functions: they were guards, messengers, and sometimes protectors or guardians. They often appeared in ethereal form, but they also appeared as humans. They were never understood to be ghosts or as people who had died and gone to heaven. At times, they were said to have light around them—the likely inspiration for the haloes that have illuminated works of art throughout the centuries.

A QUOTE FROM THE BIBLE
PSALM 91:9A, 11

The LORD Most High is your fortress … God will command his angels to protect you wherever you go.

The first mention of angels in the Bible occurs at its very beginning. Just after the story of creation, God positions angel guards at the entrance to the Garden of Eden after expelling Adam and Eve (Genesis 3). Later in Genesis, angels visit Abraham, the great ancestor of the Jewish nation. They not only tell him he will have a son in his old age, but also alert him to the coming destruction of Sodom and Gomorrah (Genesis 18). These same angels later rescue Lot and his family from a threatening mob of hostile townspeople and from the fire that destroyed the famous cities (Genesis 19).

We often think of an angel's visit as a moment of fanfare, as in the case of ancient Jacob and his memorable dream of angels going up and down a staircase or ladder (Genesis 28:10–22). Or we recall Moses encountering an angel at the burning bush (Exodus 3:1–2), or the angel that saved Daniel in the lion's den (Daniel 6:21–22), and protected his friends in the flaming furnace (Daniel 3:25-28). But there are just as many examples of angels in the most unceremonious of places. The prophet Balaam's donkey saw an angel blocking his path in the road (Numbers 22:22–35). And the unlikely warrior Gideon was hiding in a winepress when an angel sat under an oak tree to speak to him (Judges 6:11–24).

What we learn about angels from these, and many more stories of the Old Testament, is that they extend God's hand to his people. They functioned as go-betweens of sorts and were able to blend in as necessary to accomplish their work. Many questions about angels remain, though. How do they travel and communicate? Do they walk among us today as they walked among the people of the Old Testament, watching and protecting us? And if so, why do they remain hidden from our searching gaze?

Offspring of Angels?

In Genesis 6, just before the beginning of Noah's saga, the Bible speaks of "supernatural beings" that intermarried with the women in those times. The children of their union were called the Nephilim, and were a race of large people sometimes referred to as giants. Some readers have cited this biblical passage as a possible explanation for the stories of Greek mythology. Others, though, have pondered whether the supernatural beings referred to are humans gifted with seemingly superhuman strength.

Johann Liss (c.1597–1629)
Sacrifice of Isaac
Uffizi, Florence, Italy

Worshiping Angels?

For the New Testament church, much of the 1st century was spent sorting through the teachings of Jesus to agree on how to live lives of faith. Most of the literature that makes up the New Testament consists of letters written by Paul or another church leader to congregations to help them sort out such controversies. From the letter to the church at Colossae, we know that the worship of angels was one of those areas of concern (Colossians 2:18).

In John's famous apocalyptic vision, the book of Revelation, he hears as much from an angel and writes:

"My name is John, and I am the one who heard and saw these things. Then after I had heard and seen all this, I knelt down and began to worship at the feet of the angel who had shown it to me.

But the angel said, Don't do that! I am a servant, just like you. I am the same as a follower or a prophet or anyone else who obeys what is written in this book. God is the one you should worship" (Revelation 22:8–9).

Nicolas Poussin (1594–1665)
The Apotheosis of Saint Paul
Louvre, Paris, France

ANGELS
in the **new** testament

The Bible does not support the belief that people who have lived good and faithful lives become angels when they die. The line between the creatures of heaven and the creatures of earth is quite clear. Angels are a unique creation of their own, far different from men; they are seen as intermediaries between God and humans on earth.

The stories of the 1st-century church are filled with close encounters between angels and Christ's followers. When the apostles were thrown into jail for preaching the good news of Jesus Christ, an angel led them out during the night. The next day, the apostles returned to the temple courts to preach their ringing message, while the jail doors remained locked and the guards still stood at their posts (Acts 5:17–26). Later, the apostle Peter was placed in maximum security: he was not only imprisoned, but bound by chains and surrounded by guards. Suddenly an angel appeared, shed Peter of his shackles and escorted him to freedom, even as the guards who stood on either side of him were unaware of his escape (Acts 12:1–11).

An angel steered Philip, a 1st-century church leader, into the wilderness where he found an Ethiopian official struggling to comprehend a passage from Isaiah. With Philip's help, the official understood the gospel and was baptized (Acts 8:26–39).

A Roman centurion named Cornelius had a vision of an angel directing him to meet with Peter. The conversion of this important Gentile leader served as a clear indication that God's saving love was now extended to Gentiles as well as Jews.

The most exciting spectacle of angelic activity in the Bible takes place in the book of Revelation. John's vision on the island of Patmos takes him "behind the scenes" into heaven, where angels encircle the throne of God, singing his praises and performing sacred tasks at his bidding.

A QUOTE FROM THE BIBLE
ACTS 12:6–11

The night before Peter was to be put on trial, he was asleep and bound by two chains. A soldier was guarding him on each side, and two other soldiers were guarding the entrance to the jail. Suddenly an angel from the Lord appeared, and light flashed around in the cell. The angel poked Peter in the side and woke him up. Then he said, "Quick! Get up!"

The chains fell off his hands, and the angel said, "Get dressed and put on your sandals." Peter did what he was told. Then the angel said, "Now put on your coat and follow me." Peter left with the angel, but he thought everything was only a dream. They went past the two groups of soldiers, and when they came to the iron gate to the city, it opened by itself. They went out and were going along the street, when all at once the angel disappeared.

Peter now realized what had happened, and he said, "I am certain that the Lord sent his angel to rescue me from Herod and from everything the Jewish leaders planned to do to me."

ANGELS
in the life of **jesus**

The angelic appearances we read about in the Bible must have been startling, yet the celestial beings appeared to men and women in recognizable form and communicated in our tongues. Angels may not be of this world, but they certainly are able to function within it.

The birth of Jesus involved a flurry of angelic activity. According to the Bible, angels alerted the significant figures every step of the way. Even before Mary and Joseph were notified of their part in the "Christmas story," the angel Gabriel appeared to extended family member Zechariah. Zechariah would become the father of John the Baptist, the New Testament prophet who prepared the way for Jesus (Luke 1:5–25, 57–80).

A short time later, Gabriel appeared to Mary to tell her she would be chosen to give birth to God's Son (Luke 1:26–38). When Mary's fiancé, Joseph, heard the news of her pregnancy, he planned to leave her. Then an angel appeared to him in a dream with an explanation (Matthew 1:18–25). An angel directed the shepherds to the place of Jesus' birth, and a multitude of angels confirmed the message (Luke 2:8–20). Surely one of the most joyous of the many marvelous images of Christ's nativity is this heavenly host of angels that heralded his birth with song. An angel also warned Joseph in a dream to escape with his family to Egypt and then again, when it was safe, to return to Israel (Matthew 2:13–23).

Jesus' connection with heavenly angels didn't stop with his birth. Angels ministered to him after his forty-day fast and temptation in the wilderness (Matthew 4:5–11). And when faced by his enemies in Gethsemane, Jesus told his alarmed disciple Simon Peter, that if he wished, he could summon "more than twelve armies of angels" (Matthew 26:52–53).

After Jesus' crucifixion, an angel rolled the stone from the grave, causing the Roman soldiers guarding the tomb to pass out in fright (Matthew 28:1–4). Angels also announced the good news of the resurrection to the women who arrived early in the morning (Luke 24:1–8). And when Jesus ascended into heaven, two angels appeared to the disciples with the news that one day he would return in the same manner (Acts 1:6–11).

A QUOTE FROM THE BIBLE
MATTHEW 4:1, 8–11

The Holy Spirit led Jesus into the desert, so that the devil could test him . . .

Finally, the devil took Jesus up on a very high mountain and showed him all the kingdoms on earth and their power. The devil said to him, "I will give all this to you, if you will bow down and worship me."

Jesus answered, "Go away Satan! The Scriptures say: 'Worship the Lord your God and serve only him.'"

Then the devil left Jesus, and angels came to help him.

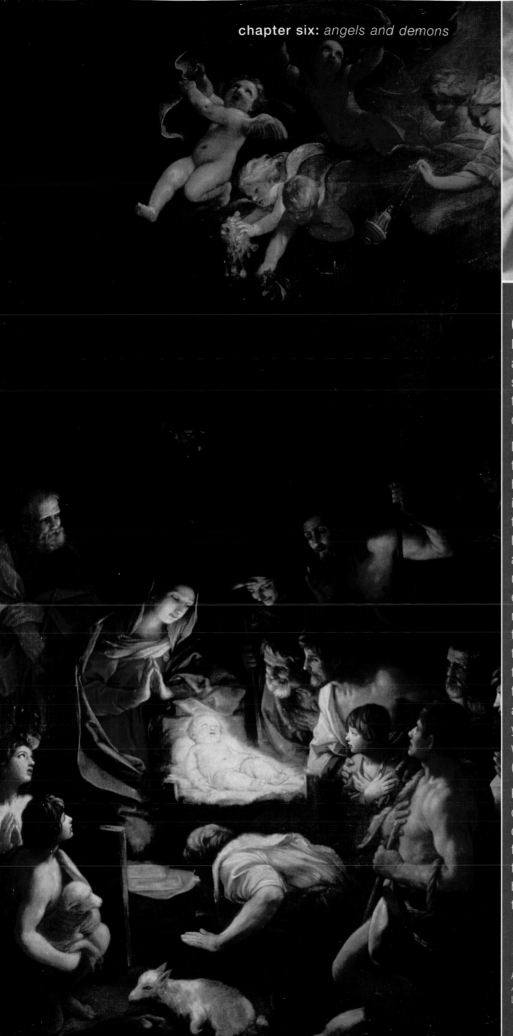

Guardian Angels

Many believe that each of us has a guardian angel assigned specifically to watch over us through life. Where did the idea of guardian angels come from?

Matthew's gospel may have fostered the idea. Jesus' disciples had come to him to ask for information about who would be the greatest in the kingdom of heaven. In answering, Jesus pulled a small child into the circle. He reminded his followers that entrance into the kingdom of God required childlike humility and faith. He then reminded them of their responsibility in influencing the innocents of their world. And finally, he said, "Don't be cruel to any of these little ones! I promise you that their angels are always with my Father in heaven" (Matthew 18:10–11).

Rather than painting the picture of angels swooping over the heads of their charges and rescuing them from danger, his words painted the picture of angels standing before God on behalf of those they protected.

Anton Raphael Mengs (1728–1779)
Adoration of the Shepherds
Location: Museo del Prado, Madrid, Spain

YOU SAID TO YOURSELF, "I'LL BE ABOVE THE CLOUDS, JUST LIKE GOD MOST HIGH…"

SATAN
fallen angel

Known by Many Names
A Jewish legend says that the first woman created was actually Lilith, who abandoned Adam and was turned into a female demon. But most of the biblical references to demons give them masculine names like Abaddon, Apollyon, Destroyer, Satan, Lucifer, and Beelzebub (literally, "lord of the flies").

Who is Satan? Many believe he was the most beautiful angel in God's heavenly choir, but he fell victim to pride and began to love himself more than he loved God; he went nose to nose with the Creator, fighting to be an equal, and he lost. Lucifer, the light bearer, had become Satan, the accuser.

The prophet Isaiah used harsh terms and vivid imagery to condemn the arrogance of the Babylonian king of his day (see citation at right). But like most prophets, he was addressing at the same time another larger, spiritual reality. This is clear in Luke 10:18 when Jesus tells his disciples, "I saw Satan fall from heaven like a flash of lightning."

For centuries, this description of Satan's fall has shaped Western writings: we find it in Dante's *Inferno* and John Milton's *Paradise Lost*. Islam teaches that Satan, or Shaitaan, refused to bow to God's new creation (Adam) and was banished from heaven. He, and other evil spirits, or jinns (the source of our term genies), remain determined to derail the righteous. Jewish tradition views Satan not only as a fallen angel, but also as God's instrument for testing humankind. All three of the Abrahamic religions agree, however, that Satan is a real being—not just a metaphor for evil. And he's bent on destruction.

Finding Satan in the Old Testament takes some sleuthing, for there are few mentions of him. In the story of Job, Satan stands before God's throne to accuse Job of hollow righteousness. More often the evil one is referred to with names like "the snake" in the Garden of Eden (Genesis 3).

The New Testament, in contrast, often mentions demons and the devil, "the god who rules this world." The message is consistent: In the realm of eternity, Satan and his minions have already lost the war, but they are no less determined to wreak destruction on God's creatures on earth.

A QUOTE FROM THE BIBLE
ISAIAH 14:12–15

You, the bright morning star,
have fallen from the sky!
You brought down other nations;
now you are brought down.
You said to yourself,
"I'll climb to heaven
and place my throne
above the highest stars.
I'll sit there with the gods
far away in the north.
I'll be above the clouds,
just like God Most High."
But now you are deep
in the world of the dead.

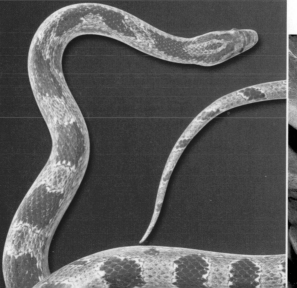

A QUOTE FROM THE BIBLE
MARK 1:23–26

Suddenly a man with an evil spirit in him entered the meeting place and yelled, "Jesus from Nazareth, what do you want with us? Have you come to destroy us? I know who you are! You are God's Holy One."

Jesus told the evil spirit, "Be quiet and come out of the man!" The spirit shook him. Then it gave a loud shout and left.

People flocked to Jesus asking him to heal the sick, the deformed— and also the demon-possessed. In one of the most dramatic New Testament encounters, a naked madman confronts Jesus and yells, "Jesus, Son of God in heaven, what do you want with me? Promise me in God's name that you won't torture me!"

Jesus asked him his name. The reply: "Legion" (which means mob) "because we are many." In other words, Jesus was not simply faced with a madman, but with a man possessed by a mob of demons. The dark spirits begged Jesus not to send them to "the pit" where demons were punished, but into a nearby herd of swine. He did so, and the possessed pigs jumped off a cliff, squealing. The townspeople, spooked by what they'd seen, mistook Christ's power over the demons as a sign of darkness and begged Jesus to leave their part of the country (Mark 5:1–20).

The Bible also tells of those who underestimated the powers of demons. As the early church was being established, many people were amazed by the healings and exorcisms they saw Jesus' apostles perform in his name. In Ephesus one group of men tried to do the same thing. They were unprepared for the strength of those they faced. The possessed man answered them back, "I know Jesus! And I have heard about Paul. But who are you?" Then he assaulted them so badly that they ran out of the building, bruised and naked (Acts 19:13–16).

Some people remain unconvinced that there are evil forces at work in the world. Is it possible, they ask, that what some call cases of demonic possession are really instances of mental illness? Movies are still made exploring the topic, and books often portray evil as merely a product of the human heart. While the thought of supernatural demons moving among us is a daunting one, the Bible clearly presents evil as a real, supernatural phenomenon.

DEMONS
an evil army

Demons Today?

If demons exist today as they did in biblical times, what would they look like? How would they behave? What weaknesses would they exploit to win humans to support their evil intentions? The noted 20th-century British writer and thinker C. S. Lewis addresses these questions in his fanciful book *The Screwtape Letters*. This novel is a fictional collection of correspondence from Screwtape, a senior level demon, to his nephew, an apprentice demon named Wormwood, who has been given a human subject to lead down the path of temptation. Lewis uses wry humor and satire to reveal the various and subtle ways in which people succumb to evil in their everyday lives.

The end of Jesus' life—his crucifixion and resurrection—are deep mysteries to ponder, yet the larger mystery of Christ begins with his very existence. After all, Jesus of Nazareth was no less than God himself, God walking the earth, breathing the air and leaving footprints in the dust. Considering that he was born the son of a carpenter, Jesus' life exceeds any other in terms of complexity and mystery.

CHAPTER

7

One of most revelatory claims of Jesus was that his power was by no means exclusive. He told his followers: "I tell you for certain that if you have faith in me, you will do the same things that I am doing. You will do even greater things, now that I am going back to the Father" (John 14:12). His words proved true after he ascended into heaven and God sent the Holy Spirit to empower and guide the church. The same powers Jesus had manifested were available to the apostles. "A lot of people living in the towns near Jerusalem brought those who were sick or troubled by evil spirits, and they were all healed." (Read Acts 5:16.)

JESUS
a life shrouded in

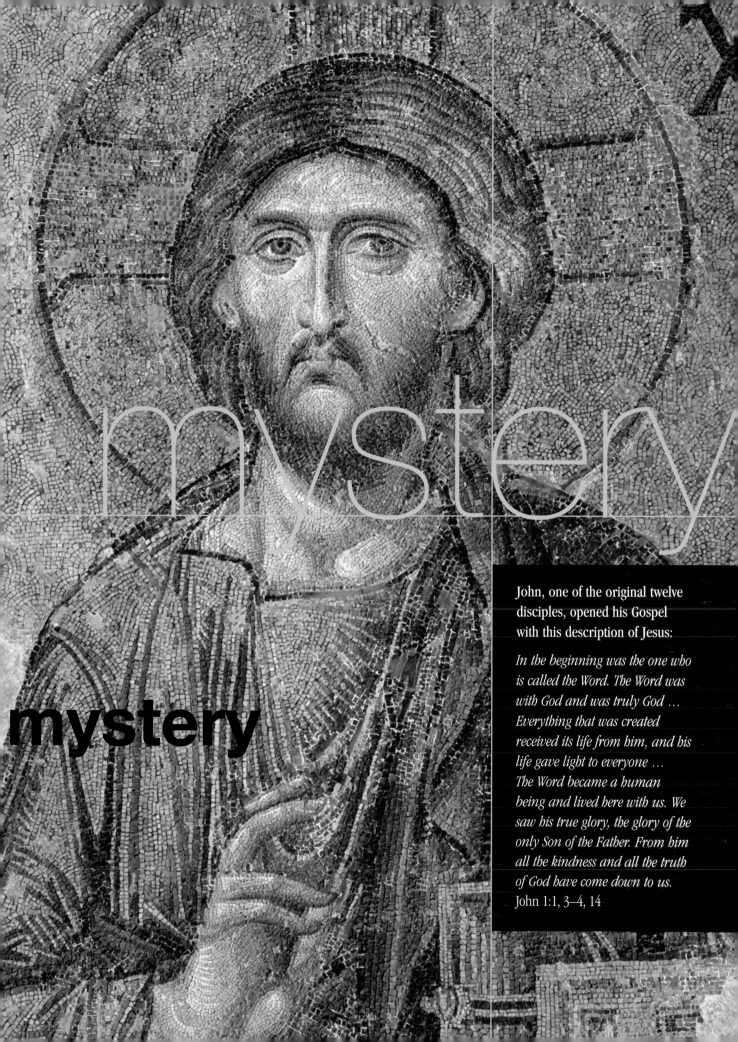

mystery

mystery

John, one of the original twelve disciples, opened his Gospel with this description of Jesus:

In the beginning was the one who is called the Word. The Word was with God and was truly God … Everything that was created received its life from him, and his life gave light to everyone … The Word became a human being and lived here with us. We saw his true glory, the glory of the only Son of the Father. From him all the kindness and all the truth of God have come down to us.
John 1:1, 3–4, 14

JESUS
mysterious **birth**

Jesus claimed to be the Messiah, God's promised Savior, sent to save people from their sins. The promise of the Messiah is told in a series of Old Testament prophecies, many of which detail the miraculous events that would surround the Savior's birth. The Messiah was to be born of a virgin (Isaiah 7:14), from the lineage of David/Jesse (Isaiah 11:1–9), in the town of Bethlehem (Micah 5:2). All these prophecies were realized in the story of Christ's nativity.

The birth of Jesus was surrounded with wonder and mystery. His earthly parents, Mary and Joseph, were prepared by personal visits from an angel. The shepherds also learned of Jesus' birth from angels.

More mysterious is the star that led the Magi, Zoroastrian astrologer-priests, to Bethlehem. How did a group of non-Jewish wise men know to respond to one particular heavenly body and leave their homes on a long journey in search of the one who had been born king of the Jews?

Angels spoke to Joseph in dreams, alerting him to danger and letting him know when it had passed (Matthew 2:13,19–20). When Mary and Joseph first presented Jesus in the temple, as was the custom, two people recognized his significance—even as an infant! They were already aware of his identity and his destiny (Luke 2:22–40). When Jesus was only 12, he could hold his own in theological discussions with the most respected religious leaders of his time (Luke 2:41–52).

When Jesus was born, he became one of us, yet the events of his birth were far more spectacular than those most of us will experience in a lifetime.

After Jesus' birth, we hear surprisingly little about him for some 30 years. Then, according to the Bible, Christ appears at the Jordan River to be baptized by John the Baptist. As he comes up out of the water, the voice of God the Father speaks from heaven: "This is my own dear Son, and I am pleased with him" (Matthew 3:17).

Soon afterward, Jesus designated the men who would become his twelve apostles and began a three-year ministry. It didn't take long for his followers to witness his startling powers:

- When a newlywed couple ran out of wine at their wedding, Jesus, at his mother's request, transformed water into wine. (John 2:1–12)
- When sickness or injury afflicted someone, Jesus could remedy the problem with a touch … or even just a word. (Matthew 9:35–38)
- Jesus walked on water and calmed storms. (Matthew 14:22–33; Mark 4:35–41)
- Jesus fed thousands with the equivalent of a child's sack lunch. (John 6:1–15)
- Blindness, physical impairments, and deafness—hardships that mysteriously afflict some people—were not insurmountable problems for Jesus. (Matthew 9:1–8; Matthew 9:27–34; Mark 7:31–37)
- Jesus healed lepers and cast demons out of numerous people. (Matthew 8:1–4; Mark 5:1–20)
- One man had been an invalid for 38 years, but had the faith and the ability to walk when Jesus told him to do so. (John 5:1–18)
- Jesus raised people from the dead. (Matthew 9:18–26; Luke 7:11–17; John 11:1–44)

Clearly, Jesus possessed extraordinary powers. So it's fascinating to note that he never uses any of the power at his disposal to make his own life easier. Once he went into the desert to pray and meditate, even going without eating for 40 days. Then Satan appeared and tempted Jesus to exert his power and turn stones into bread. But Jesus refused. On the night he was betrayed, in the Garden of Gethsemane, Jesus declared that he had 12 legions of angels (an army of 72,000) at his disposal if he wished to summon them. But he didn't; surrendering to the will of God, he never sought to escape the suffering of the cross. What Jesus chose *not* to do is often just as great a mystery as many of the miraculous things he did.

JESUS'
mysterious **life** and **ministry**

A QUOTE FROM THE BIBLE

JOHN 13:1–3, 16–17

It was before Passover, and Jesus knew that the time had come for him to leave this world and to return to the Father. He had always loved his followers in this world, and he loved them to the very end.

Even before the evening meal started, the devil had made Judas, the son of Simon Iscariot, decide to betray Jesus. Jesus knew that he had come from God and would go back to God. He also knew that the Father had given him complete power.

Jesus said to his followers . . .
"I tell you for certain that servants are not greater than their master, and messengers are not greater than the one who sent them. You know these things, and God will bless you, if you do them."

JESUS' mysterious identity

Then Jesus asked his disciples, "But who do you say

Strange Speculations

After Jesus' death, the debate continued about his identity and significance—even among those who had followed him. Strange teachings began to spread, including speculations that:

- Jesus was simply a gifted human; he was not actually God in the flesh.
- Jesus had a fully human body with a non-human, divine mind.
- Jesus didn't become divine until he had been tested by God and passed the test by living a righteous life.
- Jesus was actually two distinct people—one human and one divine.
- Jesus was merely a form of God the Father who came to earth to die on the cross for our sins.

Clearly, it was a struggle for people to understand the relationship between Jesus' humanness and his divinity. Today, we still struggle to comprehend how one person could be both fully human and fully God. The life of Jesus remains a mystery.

It's not surprising that people struggled to comprehend who Jesus really was. A carpenter's son, he passed through the local villages, healing all kinds of illnesses, casting out demons, feeding enormous crowds, and even raising the dead. Just as important, his teachings were new, revolutionary, loving, uplifting. He assured people he was not trying to do away with their law, yet his interpretation of the Scriptures was utterly new to his listeners (Matthew 5:17–18; 7:28).

As word spread about him, people began to speculate that he might be a reincarnation of John the Baptist, Elijah, Jeremiah, or one of the other ancient prophets of Israel. Jesus' opponents and doubters suggested that his power came from Beelzebub, the "lord of the flies" and prince of demons. Yet in a memorable confession after a flash of insight, Peter boldly proclaimed Jesus to be "the Messiah, the Son of the living God" (Matthew 16:16).

"What evidence is there for Jesus' divinity? The first is that of his sinless life—something only God could do. The Bible says Jesus was 'tempted in every way, just as we are—yet was without sin' (Hebrews 4:15, NIV). Then there is the evidence of his miracles—miracles that demonstrated the power of God.

"But the final proof of Jesus' divine nature was his resurrection from the dead. Anyone could claim to be the Son of God, but only Christ proved it by coming back from the grave—an event witnessed by hundreds. Who was Jesus Christ? He was God in human flesh—and he came into this world for one reason: to save us from our sins. Why not open your heart to him today?"

~Rev. Billy Graham

I am?" "You are the Messiah!" Peter replied. Mark 8:29

A QUOTE FROM THE BIBLE

"God is Spirit, and those who worship God must be led by the Spirit to worship him according to the truth."

John 4:24

JESUS
and the mystery

Perhaps one of the most mysterious aspects of Jesus' life is the way his contemporaries saw him. With very few exceptions, the extraordinary deeds and miracles he performed were public events. And when crowds of thousands are fed or lepers are healed ten at a time, it's next to impossible to keep the news from spreading.

Yet while the crowds around Galilee witnessed many of these phenomenal events, some responded with faith in his power, while others seemed determined to remain skeptical. Jesus always noticed and frequently acknowledged people's faith. And he sometimes found faith in surprising places. During Jesus' life, Judah was controlled by Rome and its militia. There was a resentment among the Jews of the soldiers' presence. Yet in one instance, a Roman soldier so impressed Jesus that he commented, "I tell you that in all of Israel I've never found anyone with this much faith!" (Matthew 8:10). It was faith that allowed Peter to walk on water, and the loss of it that caused him to begin to sink (Matthew 14:28–31). In many cases of those Jesus healed, it is the faith of the invalid that acts as a catalyst, triggering God's power.

Jesus' hometown of Nazareth was one of the places where people didn't have much faith in him (Matthew 13:53–58). For a long while, not even his own brothers believed in him (John 7:5). Yet through the mystery of faith, apparently several of them came around. It is interesting that Jesus—great teacher that he was—never wrote a book. His brothers James and Jude, however, did. The books bearing their names can be found among the General Letters in the New Testament.

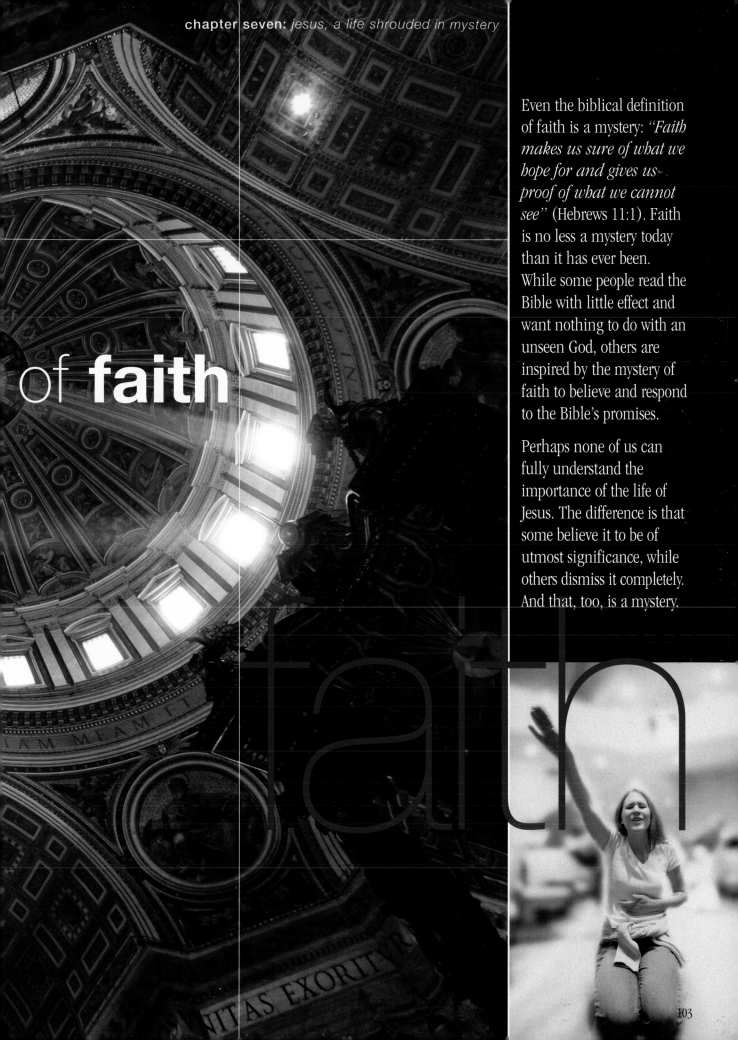

of **faith**

Even the biblical definition of faith is a mystery: *"Faith makes us sure of what we hope for and gives us proof of what we cannot see"* (Hebrews 11:1). Faith is no less a mystery today than it has ever been. While some people read the Bible with little effect and want nothing to do with an unseen God, others are inspired by the mystery of faith to believe and respond to the Bible's promises.

Perhaps none of us can fully understand the importance of the life of Jesus. The difference is that some believe it to be of utmost significance, while others dismiss it completely. And that, too, is a mystery.

CHAPTER 8

JESUS
a **death**

Was Jesus a false messiah who ended up dead? That's what some skeptics say. Others say the story of Christ's death and resurrection are merely metaphorical, symbols of our soul's salvation if we follow Christ's path. But the writers of the Gospels clearly state that Jesus died on the cross and quote witnesses who saw him after he rose from the dead.

A myriad of hypotheses attempt to account for why Jesus' body went missing after his death. The most famous of these is the "swoon theory," which suggests Jesus didn't die on the cross, but merely passed out and revived later in the tomb. Another explanation is that the disciples, overcome by grief and disoriented in the dark of night, returned to the wrong tomb and only thought they saw angels there. Christianity, however, anchors its existence on the historical fact of Jesus' actual resurrection. So, what exactly does the New Testament say about it?

Four books of the New Testament record the story of Jesus' crucifixion in their final pages: The Gospel writers Matthew and John presented themselves as disciples of Jesus, Mark was a close friend of the disciple Peter; and Luke was a first-century doctor, writer, and historian who took pride in his abilities to check facts accurately.

The details vary slightly in each of these accounts, so readers, like jurors at a trial, often examine the differences between the stories in order to reach a more complete understanding of the events described. Importantly, however, the key elements of each of these four books agree: Jesus' death was accompanied by inexplicable natural phenomena.

even more mysterious

a life **foretold**

Christians believe that many of the Old Testament prophecies concerning the Messiah—as many as 300 to 500 of them—were fulfilled through Jesus' life, death, and resurrection.

The Messiah was to be	Jesus fulfilled the prophecy in
born of a virgin	
Isaiah 7:14	Matthew 1:21–23
a descendant of Abraham	
Genesis 12:1–3; 22:1	Matthew 1:1; Luke 3:34
of the tribe of Judah	
Genesis 49:10	Luke 3:33
of the house of David	
2 Samuel 7:12–16; Jeremiah 33:14–16	Matthew 1:1; Luke 1:32; 3:31
born in Bethlehem	
Micah 5:2	Matthew 2:1–6; Luke 2:4–7
taken to Egypt	
Hosea 11:1	Matthew 2:13–15
heralded by a messenger	
Isaiah 40:3–5; Malachi 3:1	Matthew 3:1–3; Mark 1:1–3; Luke 3:1–6

What are the chances that one man could fulfill even eight of the prophecies of the Messiah?

In 1969, a mathematician named Peter W. Stoner gave his students eight prophecies that were fulfilled by Christ and asked the students to figure the probability of their all being fulfilled. The prophecies he chose stated that the Messiah would …

❶ Be born in Bethlehem
❷ Be preceded by a messenger
❸ Ride on a donkey
❹ Be betrayed by a friend
❺ Be betrayed for thirty pieces of silver
❻ Be betrayed for money used to purchase the potter's field
❼ Be silent as a lamb
❽ Have his hands and feet pierced

The class came up with a whopping number: the combined probability of one person's fulfilling eight of the Old Testament prophecies would be one chance in 10^{17}. (Yes, that's a one followed by seventeen zeroes.) And since the initial finding by Stoner's students, his grandson Don has updated the number to 10^{18}, since the world's population is now larger. (See www.geocities.com/stonerdon/ science_speaks.html.)

Jesus himself said, "Everything written about me in the Law of Moses, the Books of the Prophets, and in the Psalms had to happen" (Luke 24:44).

The Messiah would	Jesus fulfilled the prophecy in
enter Jerusalem on a donkey Zechariah 9:9	Matthew 21:6–11; Luke 19:28–38; John 12:12–15
be betrayed by a friend Psalm 41:9; 55:12–14	Matthew 26:20–25, 47–50; Luke 22:3–6; John 13:18–30
be betrayed for thirty pieces of silver Zechariah 11:12–13	Matthew 26:14–16; 27:3–10
be silent as a lamb before his accusers Isaiah 53:7	Matthew 27:12–14; Mark 15:3–5
be crucified, with his hands, feet, and side pierced Psalm 22:16; Zechariah 12:10	Luke 24:39; John 19:18, 34–37; 20:20–28
thirst on the cross and be given drugged wine or vinegar Psalm 69:21	Matthew 27:34; Mark 15:23; Luke 23:36; John 19:29
see lots cast for his garments Psalm 22:18	Matthew 27:35; Mark 15:24; John 19:23–24
die with transgressors Isaiah 53:8–12	Matthew 27:38; Mark 15:27; Luke 22:37; 23:32–33
be buried by a rich man Isaiah 53:9	Matthew 27:57–60; Mark 15:42–46; Luke 23:50–53
rise from the dead Psalm 16:10	Matthew 28:5–6; Mark 16:6; Luke 24:5–7; Acts 2:31

JESUS
phenomena surrounding the **crucifixion**

What exactly happened on the day Jesus was put to death—the day many Christians call Good Friday?

Darkness Fell in the Middle of the Day

All three Synoptic Gospel writers claim that, around noon on Good Friday, the sky darkened and remained dark until 3 p.m. (Matthew 27:45; Mark 15:33; Luke 23:44—45). Around eight hundred years before Christ was crucified, the ancient prophet Amos had written, "On that day, I, the LORD God, will make the sun go down at noon, and I will turn daylight into darkness" (Amos 8:9). Looking back through history, many make the connection between this prophecy and the strange darkness that fell upon Jerusalem on the day of Christ's death.

The Ground Shook

Matthew wrote that "the earth shook, and rocks split apart" at the time of Jesus' death (Matthew 27:51—52). He also recorded that, in response to this earthquake, the officer and soldiers on guard exclaimed, "This man really was God's Son!" (Matthew 27:54).

Tombs Opened and the Dead Walked

According to Matthew, when Jesus died, there were others who actually *rose* from the dead. By the time Jesus left the tomb three days later, these people, previously dead and buried, walked into Jerusalem and were seen by those who knew them (Matthew 27:52–53). When Matthew wrote his account, some of these people and their relatives most likely were still alive. He probably wouldn't have risked including mention of this miraculous occurrence if it hadn't actually happened.

The Curtain of the Temple Was Torn

According to New Testament writers Matthew, Mark, and Luke, at the moment Jesus died, a curtain in the temple ripped from top to bottom. This heavy curtain of Herod's temple hung like a door between the worshipers outside and the most holy place—considered the dwelling place of God (Matthew 27:51; Mark 15:38; Luke 23:45).

This event symbolized the dramatic change that had been accomplished by Jesus' death on the cross: his sacrifice shattered old barriers between sinful humans and their holy Creator and opened a new pathway that allows us to experience peace and communion with God.

Death on the Cross

Crucifixion was first employed as a form of capital punishment by the Persians and was later adopted by the Egyptians, Carthaginians, and Romans. It was deliberately designed to lead to a death that was not only humiliating to the victim, but also extremely painful and lengthy—as Mel Gibson's film *The Passion of the Christ* illustrated in gruesome detail.

Though many illustrations of the crucifixion of Christ show him fixed to the cross by nails driven into his hands, as in the small picture at left, contemporary scholars believe victims were more likely affixed to the cross by nails driven through the wrists, which were better able to support a victim's weight.

Roman historians tell us that after Spartacus and his band of rebel slaves were captured by the authorities in 71 BC, some 6,000 of them were crucified along both sides of the Appian Way. The bodies were left to rot on their crosses, as a sign of the fate that would meet any slave rebellions in the future.

After Jesus died, Joseph of Arimathea—a rich Jewish leader in Jerusalem who was a secret follower of Jesus—requested the body. Nicodemus, another high-placed follower of Christ, whose conversation with Jesus is recorded in John 3, accompanied Joseph. Together they placed the body in the rock tomb that Joseph had planned to be used for his own burial. Then they secured the opening to the tomb with a large, heavy stone, which may have weighed as much as two tons.

JESUS
the **empty tomb**

The Roman Guards

After Jesus was buried, the authorities who had demanded his execution went back to ask the governor to place Roman guards outside the tomb because they feared Jesus' followers might attempt to steal the body (Matthew 27: 62–66). The guards placed an official seal of Rome on the stone door to the tomb.

Could Christ's followers have taken the body? It would have been difficult. Roman soldiers found guilty of leaving their posts were generally put to death. And it was common knowledge that the penalty for breaking a Roman seal was execution. Disciples bent on body-snatching would first have had to overpower the battle-tested Roman soldiers, then break the Roman seal. Yet even if they succeeded they would face a final challenge: moving aside the two-ton stone door that covered the entrance to the rock tomb.

The First Easter Morning

When two of Jesus' followers, Mary Magdalene and another woman named Mary, arrived on Easter Sunday morning, they found the mammoth stone had been rolled away from the tomb—where an angel wearing a bright white robe now sat. The Roman soldiers appeared to be dead (Matthew 28:1–4). But the soldiers, it turned out, were only stunned, and the authorities bribed them to spread the false rumor that Jesus' body had been stolen (Matthew 28:11-15).

According to John's account, when Mary Magdalene saw that the stone had been rolled away from the entrance, she raced back to tell the other disciples, two of whom then ran to the tomb to see for themselves. John got there first and saw the burial cloth lying flat inside the empty tomb (John 20:1–5).

Jesus had risen from the dead!

JESUS
the **resurrection**

Peter Paul Rubens (1577–1640)
Koninklijk Museum voor Schone Kunsten,
Antwerp, Belgium

A QUOTE FROM THE BIBLE
JOHN 20:26–28

A week later the disciples were together again. This time, Thomas was with them. Jesus came in while the doors were still locked and stood in the middle of the group. He greeted his disciples and said to Thomas, "Put your finger here and look at my hands! Put your hand into my side. Stop doubting and have faith!"

Thomas replied, "You are my Lord and my God!"

and the **life**

Eyewitnesses of the Resurrected Christ

According to the New Testament, hundreds of eyewitnesses saw Jesus alive after the resurrection. They included Mary Magdalene and other women who had followed Jesus, the surviving disciples, two discouraged men on the road to Emmaus, and more than five hundred other followers who saw Christ at another gathering.

The resurrected Jesus took on a new form, being able to move through walls and vanish at will. And he wasn't always recognizable, even to those who knew him well. Yet he was no bodiless spirit. In fact, Mary Magdalene, the first person to encounter him, mistook him for a gardener. Right after the resurrection, the disciples had locked themselves in a room to hide from Jewish leaders, when suddenly Jesus appeared in their midst. He said, "Touch me and find out for yourselves. Ghosts don't have flesh and bones as you see I have" (Luke 24:39). He even ate food in their presence—roasted fish and bread (John 21:13).

Even though Jesus' resurrected body functioned outside of typical human limitations, it still bore the scars from the crucifixion: the nail prints in his hands and feet, and the spear wound in his side. When Jesus first appeared to the disciples, all except Thomas were there and recognized Jesus because of the unmistakable scars.

When told the news that the Savior had been resurrected, Thomas said, "I must put my hand where the spear went into his side. I won't believe unless I do this!" (John 20:25). It was from this demand that Thomas came to be known as a doubter. Yet, when he saw Jesus, who invited him to touch his wounds, Thomas recognized him without ever making a move.

Jesus Ascends to Heaven

Luke, the writer of both the gospel of Luke and the book of Acts, recorded the last time the disciples saw Jesus on earth: "[Jesus] raised his hands and blessed them. As he was doing this, he left and was taken up to heaven" (Luke 24:50–51). "While they were watching, he was taken up into a cloud" (Acts 1:9).

Prior to his death, Jesus told his followers that he would be leaving them, but he promised that he would send the Holy Spirit to comfort and guide them (John 14:16–17). He gave them parting instructions to carry on his work throughout the world (Matthew 28:18–20; Luke 24:45–49).

Two Resurrections

While Jesus was still alive, he raised his good friend Lazarus from the dead. When he did so, Jesus stood outside the tomb and

called to Lazarus to come out of his stone tomb. When Lazarus complied, dumbfounding the crowd of mourners who had already been outside the tomb for days, he was still wrapped in his grave clothes. Jesus gave instructions to the crowd to help him out of the strips of cloth in which corpses were generally wrapped from head to foot in those times (John 11).

In the case of Jesus' resurrection, however, the strips of cloth were lying in the tomb. And the cloth that had been around Jesus' head wasn't lying haphazardly on the ground. It had been rolled up and placed deliberately aside (John 20:6–7).

CHAPTER 9

more than
smoke &

Bushes that burn with a consuming flame—yet remain unconsumed. A gigantic, fearsome warrior—towering almost 10 feet tall—humbled by a poor shepherd boy's slingshot. Handwriting burnt into walls by a flaming, disembodied hand. Sandals that don't wear out, even after 40 years of wandering in the desert.

The Bible is a book of wonders and marvels. Here are tales that defy nature's laws, challenge our preconceptions, turn logic upside down and, again and again, test our belief in what is possible.

And that's the point, of course. For the stories in the Bible are tales of faith, not reason; they are directed not to our brains, but to our spirits. They challenge us to believe in the power of faith, a power that makes all things possible.

The Bible is written in the language of mystery. But this is not the smoke-and-mirrors magic of a Las Vegas performer; it's the deeper, spiritual mystery of God's will at work in the world.

mirrors

MATTHEW 17:14–21

Jesus and his disciples returned to the crowd. A man knelt in front of him and said, "Lord, have pity on my son! He has a bad case of epilepsy and often falls into a fire or into water. I brought him to your disciples, but none of them could heal him."

Jesus said, "You people are too stubborn to have any faith! How much longer must I be with you? Why do I have to put up with you? Bring the boy here." Then Jesus spoke sternly to the demon. It went out of the boy, and right then he was healed.

Later the disciples went to Jesus in private and asked him, "Why couldn't we force out the demon?"

Jesus replied: "It is because you don't have enough faith! But I can promise you this. If you had faith no larger than a mustard seed, you could tell this mountain to move from here to there. And it would. Everything would be possible for you."

the burning bush

A QUOTE FROM THE BIBLE
EXODUS 3:1–6

One day, Moses was taking care of the sheep and goats of his father-in-law Jethro, the priest of Midian, and Moses decided to lead them across the desert to Sinai, the holy mountain. There an angel of the LORD appeared to him from a burning bush. Moses saw that the bush was on fire, but it was not burning up. "This is strange!" he said to himself. "I'll go over and see why the bush isn't burning up." When the LORD saw Moses coming near the bush, he called him by name, and Moses answered, "Here I am." God replied, "Don't come any closer. Take off your sandals—the ground where you are standing is holy. I am the God who was worshiped by your ancestors Abraham, Isaac, and Jacob." Moses was afraid to look at God, and so he hid his face.

Just as the Bible is a book of marvels, it is a book of symbols. And surely among the most memorable of the great book's symbols is the incandescent moment when God first speaks to Moses in the form of a burning bush, summoning him to a life of service and faith.

Why did God choose to appear as a flame, a fire burning endlessly, without consuming the fuel that feeds its flames? After all, God could have chosen many avenues to speak to Moses: he could have appeared as a figure in a dream, or a voice in a vision. He might have taken the form of a simple pilgrim on the road.

But God chose to appear in the form of fire, a symbol of power and life. Embodied in a bush that burned without consuming itself, God took the symbolic form of the very quality he was calling on Moses to summon: faith. For spiritual faith, like a burning bush, is an internal flame that burns endlessly, yet constantly renews itself.

In the burning bush, Moses saw God's power over natural forces. But he also saw an unforgettable symbol of the endlessly replenishing power of faith.

Vision of a Promised Land

When God spoke to Moses in the form of a burning bush, he reaffirmed that the Jews were his Chosen People and he offered Moses a vision of the future home of the Jews what they began calling the Promised Land : "I will bring my people out of Egypt into a country where there is good land, rich with milk and honey. I will give them the land where the Canaanites, Hittites, Amorites, Perizzites, Hivites, and Jebusites now live. My people have begged for my help, and I have seen how cruel the Egyptians are to them. Now go to the king! I am sending you to lead my people out of his country" (Exodus 2:7-10).

Statue of Moses and the Ten Commandments in Copenhagen at Our Lady's Church

Moses' Shining Face

The people of Moses' day were afraid they would die if they stood in God's presence. From Moses' experience, it was obvious that to experience God's power was to allow oneself to be utterly transformed. When Moses spoke to God, his face would glow so brightly afterward that his fellow Israelites were afraid—so much so that Moses began covering his face with a veil when he spoke to them (Exodus 34:33).

When God created the heavens and earth, his first words were, "Let there be light!" When we encounter God as did Moses, the result is illumination.

written in

Michelangelo was one of the great painters of the Renaissance. Yet his first love was not painting, but sculpture; while his pigments and frescoes might fade, he knew that marble would weather the ravages of time.

When John Keats sought an image for the enduring power of art, he found it not in a book or a painting, but in a marble Grecian urn. "When old age shall this generation waste," he wrote, "Thou shalt remain."

When 20th-century sculptor Gustav Borglum sought to create a monument to American presidents that would endure for the ages, he transformed an entire mountain—Mount Rushmore—into his canvas.

And when God sought a symbol for the enduring power of the Ten Commandments that would guide his chosen people, he sought, above all, a sign of permanence. His commandments would not be written on papyrus, to decay and wither; they would be chiseled in stone. These Commandments were written to last, as meaningful for believers three thousand years in the future as they were for Moses, the man who first beheld them. Long before the days of Marshall McLuhan (Canadian philosopher and communications theorist, 1911–1980), God knew that for these enduring guideposts of moral life, the medium was the message.

Stone endures, as Jesus knew when he declared that his apostle Peter would be "the rock" upon which Christianity would be built (Matthew 16:18).

Yet there is a final irony in this story in the medium used for the Ten Commandments. For though they were carved by the hand of God onto tablets of stone, the intended resting place of the Ten Commandments is that most evanescent, if eternal, of locations: the human spirit. Centuries later, God, speaking to the people through the prophet Jeremiah, said: "I will write my laws on their hearts and minds" (Jeremiah 31:33).

stone

A QUOTE FROM THE BIBLE
EXODUS 34:29–30

Moses came down from Mount Sinai, carrying the Ten Commandments. His face was shining brightly because the LORD had been speaking to him… When Aaron and the others looked at Moses, they saw that his face was shining, and they were afraid to go near him.

"The true work of art is but a shadow of the divine perfection."
Michelangelo

The Lord works in strange ways. And maybe the Lord was indulging his sense of humor when he decided to announce his presence to the prophet Balaam through a most unusual mouthpiece indeed—Balaam's donkey.

According to Numbers 22, Balak, the king of Moab, had become desperate to drive away the Israelites, who had settled near his territory after their 40 years of wandering in the desert. And Balak had every reason to be concerned. The battle-hardened Hebrews had already conquered the armies of two kings in the region: Sihon, king of the Amorites, and Og, king of Bashan. Realizing that his new neighbors had become too strong to defeat, the king decided to ask the greatest prophet in his land, Balaam, to curse them, and he sent messengers to deliver his request.

Balaam received the men, but when he conferred with God, he learned that the Israelites had already been blessed by God. He knew then that he would not be allowed to curse them. So Balaam refused the king's messengers. Soon, however, they returned with an even more enticing offer of compensation. Balaam refused again, saying that no amount of money would convince him to defy the orders of his God. Finally, God did allow him to go with the men, but with specific instructions.

As they traveled to Moab the next day, Balaam's donkey suddenly halted in the road, locked his legs, dug in his hooves, and refused to go forward—the very picture of stubbornness. Balaam beat the animal and urged it on through a vineyard, but the donkey balked and pinned Balaam's foot against a fence. Again Balaam beat the animal. Finally, the beast lay down right where it was. It was then that the donkey looked Balaam in the eye and spoke to him: "What have I done to you that made you beat me three times?" (Numbers 22:28).

Now, if you found yourself addressed by a donkey, you might be struck speechless with alarm. Not Balaam: he not only talked back to the donkey—he argued with him. Only then did God open Balaam's eyes to see the source of the donkey's distress. Balaam had been so distracted by the talk of great riches and King Balak's plight that he had been blind to God's angel, who was now standing in his way, swinging a mighty sword. The angel allowed Balaam to proceed to Moab, but reminded him of his instructions: to speak only what was spoken to him, nothing more.

How can a donkey talk? One explanation might be that Balaam, as a prophet, "heard" what his donkey was attempting to communicate, even though it might have sounded like regular braying to anyone else. Yet the New Testament says Balaam's donkey "spoke to him with a human voice and made him stop his foolishness" (2 Peter 2:16).

The Bible is a book of mysteries and marvels. And is it any less a mystery that Balaam's eyes were opened to see an angel than that his donkey's mouth was opened to speak? Or that even a holy man might be so swayed by the riches of this earth as to ignore the voice of God? Either way, it must have been a shock for the prophet to realize that he lacked the depth of spiritual insight God had given to the humble beast he was riding.

Balaam and his ass stopped by an angel.
Paris, 1253-1270.
From the Psalter of St. Louis, MS Latin 10525, fol 39r.
Bibliotheque Nationale, Paris, France

A QUOTE FROM THE BIBLE
NUMBERS 22:22–27

Balaam was riding his donkey to Moab, and two of his servants were with him. But God was angry that Balaam had gone, so one of the LORD's angels stood in the road to stop him. When Balaam's donkey saw the angel standing there with a sword, it walked off the road and into an open field. Balaam had to beat the donkey to get it back on the road.

Then the angel stood between two vineyards, in a narrow path with a stone wall on each side. When the donkey saw the angel, it walked so close to one of the walls that Balaam's foot scraped against the wall. Balaam beat the donkey again.

The angel moved once more and stood in a spot so narrow that there was no room for the donkey to go around. So it just lay down. Balaam lost his temper, then picked up a stick and smacked the donkey.

Balaam in the News

In 1967, an archaeological dig in Jordan revealed an inscription made in red and black ink on plaster walls. It described a prophecy from something called the book of Balaam. Balaam was described as the son of Beor, as is the Balaam we read about in the book of Numbers. In this prophecy, however, he is further described as a prophet for Shamash, the sun god worshiped by the Babylonians and Sumerians.

a donkey talks

The infant Samuel being offered to the high priest Eli.
Gothic manuscript. 15th CE.
Bibliotheque Nationale, Paris, France

called by name

God in the Old Testament spoke in many ways and appeared in many forms to those he addressed.

He startled Moses by appearing in the form of a burning bush. He communicated the Ten Commandments to the Israelites by engraving them—in his own hand—in solid rock. Perhaps there was a touch of humor in his treatment of Balaam, a prophet of the kingdom of Moab, for God spoke to Balaam through a long-eared, four-footed interlocutor: a donkey.

Yet when God wanted to speak to Samuel, he spoke directly. Perhaps this was a sign of Samuel's special significance, for this great leader and prophet was the link between two important eras in the history of the Israelites. Samuel was the last of the judges of Israel and the man who would one day anoint Saul and David, the first two kings of Israel.

Samuel's close encounter with God began when he was still a child, serving as an assistant in the tabernacle. It was there that God first spoke to him, calling his name in the night.

The Bible says that Samuel lived in a time when dreams and visions were rare, and God no longer seemed to speak to his people. These were dark times for the Israelites: their enemies the Philistines kept them in subjection.

So when Samuel heard someone calling his name in the darkness, he ran to his guardian, the old priest Eli, to see what he needed. "Here I am. What do you want?" he asked the priest. But the old man sent him back to bed.

A short while later Samuel heard the voice again, and again he went to Eli, who dismissed him. But the third time Samuel came to his room, the old priest realized what was happening: this was no dream, no figment of the imagination. For the first time in years, the voice of God was being heard in the land of Israel.

Eli instructed Samuel to acknowledge the voice that was calling to him from the darkness and listen carefully to what God had to say.

The Lord's message was stern: Eli and his two sons, Hophni and Phinehas, were wicked. They had failed in their priestly duties. As a result, woe would be visited upon the land.

And so it was that the Israelites rose in rebellion against the Philistines, only to lose two mighty battles. But they lost something far more precious than a battle: the Philistines seized the Ark of the Covenant, the most sacred vessel of the Hebrews.

When the old priest Eli heard the news, he fell from his chair, broke his neck, and died. His sons were struck down for their wickedness. But God raised up Samuel—who had heard his voice and heeded his call—and made him the foremost leader of Israel. In time, Samuel would lead the Israelites to victory over the Philistines.

A QUOTE FROM THE BIBLE
1 SAMUEL 3:1–11

Samuel served the LORD by helping Eli the priest, who was by that time almost blind. In those days, the LORD hardly ever spoke directly to people, and he did not appear to them in dreams very often. But one night, Eli was asleep in his room, and Samuel was sleeping on a mat near the sacred chest in the LORD's house. They had not been asleep very long when the LORD called out Samuel's name. "Here I am!" Samuel answered. Then he ran to Eli and said, "Here I am. What do you want?"

"I didn't call you," Eli answered. "Go back to bed.". . .

The LORD had not spoken to Samuel before, and Samuel did not recognize the voice . . .

Eli finally realized that it was the LORD who was speaking to Samuel. So he said, "Go back and lie down! If someone speaks to you again, answer, 'I'm listening, LORD. What do you want me to do?' "

Once again Samuel went back and lay down.

The LORD then stood beside Samuel and called out as he had done before, "Samuel! Samuel!"

"I'm listening," Samuel answered. "What do you want me to do?"

The LORD said: "Samuel, I am going to do something in Israel that will shock everyone who hears about it!"

the handwriting on the wall

מנא מנא תקל ופרסן

Belshazzar reads the handwriting on the wall written by the finger of God.

124

Taken captive as a young man by the Babylonians, Daniel became a chief advisor, prophet and interpreter of dreams. Through the cunning of his rivals, he was cast into a den of lions and three of his colleagues were thrown into a fiery furnace—ordeals they survived through God's grace.

Though God never speaks directly to Daniel in the Bible, he employs Daniel as the translator through whom a terrible message and a terrible fate are visited upon those who mock the Lord.

Daniel was an Israelite, born in Jerusalem to one of the noble families of the kingdom of Judah. In these times, the days of the Babylonian Captivity, the Israelites were subservient to the Assyrians under King Nebuchadnezzar. Daniel and three other noble youths were taken to Babylon, Nebuchadnezzar's capital, as hostages. There they were trained in the pagan arts by the magi, the astrologer-priests—yet they remained loyal to the God of Israel.

Daniel rose high in the councils of Babylon, and demonstrated a gift for interpreting dreams and visions. So it was natural that when God spoke to the court of Nebuchadnezzar's son, King Belshazzar, in a most mysterious way, Daniel would be called in to translate.

The story of Belshazzar's feast is one of the great scenes of the Bible: with the army of Cyrus the Persian threatening the city, Belshazzar and a host of his nobles and their concubines descended into debauchery, reveling in an enormous, drunken feast.

At the height of the party, Belshazzar called for the sacred vessels of the Israelites, stolen when Solomon's Temple in Jerusalem was sacked. He and his cohorts drank wine from them, even as they sang the praises of their pagan gods and roared over the fate of the fallen Hebrews.

Yet every tongue fell silent when, out of nowhere, a hand appeared and wrote four words on the wall of the chamber: *Mene, mene, tekel, parsin*. Then, as quickly as it had appeared, the mysterious hand vanished.

No one could read the words: what could they mean? And by whose will were they written? Finally, Daniel was summoned to the room. The words, he told Belshazzar, were a severe sentence upon his head: the king had been weighed in the balance by God and had been found wanting. His kingdom would be divided; it could not stand.

And so it came to pass. That very night Belshazzar was slain, and the Persians conquered Babylon.

Once again, God had chosen to communicate with our world. The hand that wrote his words may have seemed an illusion, but the message it wrought was all too real.

A QUOTE FROM THE BIBLE
DANIEL 5:25–31

The words written there are *mene,* which means "numbered," *tekel,* which means "weighed," and *parsin,* which means "divided." God has numbered the days of your kingdom and has brought it to an end. He has weighed you on his balance scales, and you fall short of what it takes to be king. So God has divided your kingdom between the Medes and the Persians. Belshazzar gave a command for Daniel to be made the third most powerful man in his kingdom and to be given a purple robe and a gold chain.

That same night, the king was killed. Then Darius the Mede, who was sixty-two years old, took over his kingdom.

Persian and Medean warriors. Relief from the Audience Hall of Darius I (Apadana), eastern stairway. Achaemenid dynasty, 6th–5th c. BCE. Persepolis, Iran

CHAPTER 10

STRANGE

In the early years of the 11th century, England's King Canute grew weary of the flattery of fawning courtiers. When they dared tell him that even the sea would obey his mandates, he decided that actions speak louder than words: the king had his servants carry his royal chair to the seaside as the tide rolled in.

BUT TRUE

There sat Canute, boldly commanding the waves to stop. Yet in rolled the breakers, crashing against the shore until small waves were licking at his feet. Canute's attendants were forced into an embarrassed silence. The monarch had made his point: only one King has the power to control the earth and the waters.

Again and again, the Bible attests to God's power over creation. At God's command, waters part, stormy seas grow calm, a few loaves and fish become many (enough to nourish a throng). Even the oil left in a clay jar is replenished. The message: where there is faith, God's miracles make a way.

A QUOTE FROM THE BIBLE
LUKE 17:5–6

The apostles said to the Lord, "Make our faith stronger!"

Jesus replied: "If you had faith no bigger than a tiny mustard seed, you could tell this mulberry tree to pull itself up, roots and all, and to plant itself in the ocean. And it would!"

PARTING THE WATERS

crossing the **red sea**

Recent events provide eloquent testimony to the devastating power of water. A tsunami in the Indian Ocean killed more than 225,000 people late in 2004. Nine months later, Hurricane Katrina transformed one of America's most historic cities into swampland—only a year after a murderer's row of four major hurricanes battered residents of Florida and the Gulf Coast.

Here are powers that dwarf those of men, that reduce our works to child's toys. In the face of a hurricane's raging winds, even our levees, dams, and canals offer no more protection than did the feeble cries of King Canute against the tide.

Yet one power transcends even that of tsunamis and hurricanes. Some of the most memorable stories of the Old Testament offer chilling descriptions of nature's law suspended, as the forces of mass, gravity, and inertia heed the commands of God and his prophets.

Moses Parts the Red Sea

After the plagues devastated Egypt, Pharaoh not only allowed the Israelites to leave, he demanded that they do so. But his royal anger quickly subsided, and realizing that he was losing his slave population, Pharaoh sent his army to retrieve them.

With the entire Egyptian army on their heels and the Red Sea spread out before them, the Israelites were trapped, and panic quickly spread. At God's command, Moses held his staff over the waters and the sea parted, rising in two towering liquid walls with a path of dry ground between them. The Israelites quickly passed through, while the army that followed was swallowed up as the waters returned to their natural state. (Read Exodus 14.)

Aristotle observed that, "Water seeks its own level." By that he meant that water wasn't able to stand up in huge walls—at least, not in its liquid state. And freezing temperatures to form ice walls weren't very likely in the desert climate of Egypt. So how did the Red Sea crossing occur? A BBC documentary posed these possibilities:

■ An enormous volcanic explosion on a Greek island might have created walls of water that were witnessed and incorporated into the story of the exodus.
■ A tectonic uplift (a shelf of land rising near shore just beneath the water's surface) might have created dry ground with water on either side. This unusual occurrence would have been aided by strong winds—and a strong east wind is mentioned in the biblical account.
■ The pillar of fire leading the Israelites, the parting of the water, and the death of the Egyptians may all have been the work of extraterrestrials. But the Bible is a story of human suffering and salvation; to attribute its miracles to UFOs is to mock its meaning.

If these explanations sound implausible, well, they should. If miracles could be explained by natural law, they wouldn't be miracles.

A QUOTE FROM THE BIBLE
EXODUS 14:19–22

All this time God's angel had gone ahead of Israel's army, but now he moved behind them. A large cloud had also gone ahead of them, but now it moved between the Egyptians and the Israelites. The cloud gave light to the Israelites, but made it dark for the Egyptians, and during the night they could not come any closer.

Moses stretched his arm over the sea, and the LORD sent a strong east wind that blew all night until there was dry land where the water had been. The sea opened up, and the Israelites walked through on dry land with a wall of water on each side.

The Jordan River, which empties into the Dead Sea, meanders through many of the most memorable stories of the Bible. In the days of Joshua, the river flowed along the eastern border of Canaan, the region the Israelites considered their Promised Land. In order to complete their conquest, however, they would have to cross over the river.

Joshua Halts the Jordan

Forty years after the Red Sea crossing, Joshua (who had succeeded Moses as leader of the Israelites) was ready to cross the flooded Jordan River in order to enter Canaan, the land God had promised the Israelites. He ordered the priests to lift the sacred chest (Ark of the Covenant), which represented God's special bond with his chosen people, and step out into the waters.

The people must have feared the worst. Yet as soon as the waters touched the feet of the priests, they began to gather upstream and a miraculous silence came over the land as the raging river stopped flowing. The priests stood holding the Ark in the dry riverbed while the Israelites crossed. As soon as all the people, including the priests, were safely on the other side, the waters returned to their original state. (Read Joshua 3—4.)

The Jordan Is Tamed Again

Centuries later, the great prophet Elijah and his apprentice, Elisha, also parted the waters of the Jordan. Unlike Moses and Joshua, Elijah had neither a staff to raise nor a sacred Ark to command the stream. No matter: he simply rolled up his own cloak and struck the water with it. The river immediately divided into two walls, and he and Elisha walked across on dry ground.

More wonders followed: the Bible then says that Elijah was taken up into heaven by a chariot of fire, appearing out of a whirlwind. After he passed from sight, Elisha saw his teacher's cloak lying on the ground, a symbol that Elijah's work was now his. Elisha struck the water again with the cloak, and the waters parted for him to walk back across the Jordan. All those watching then knew God had granted him the power and authority to follow in Elijah's footsteps. (Read 2 Kings 1:1–18.)

A QUOTE FROM THE BIBLE
JOSHUA 3:1–5

Early the next morning, Joshua and the Israelites packed up and left Acacia. They went to the Jordan River and camped there that night. Two days later their leaders went through the camp, shouting, "When you see some of the priests carrying the sacred chest, you'll know it is time to cross to the other side. You've never been there before, and you won't know the way, unless you follow the chest. But don't get too close! Stay about half a mile back."

Joshua told the people, "Make yourselves acceptable to worship the LORD, because he is going to do some amazing things for us"

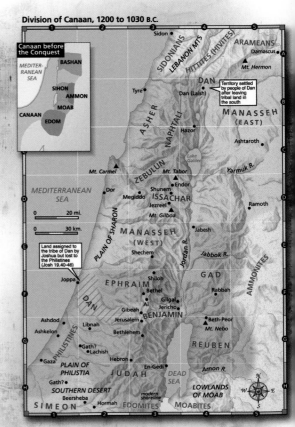

Division of Canaan, 1200 to 1030 B.C.

James Jacques Joseph Tissot (1836-1902) and Followers.
The Ark Passes over Jordan.
The Jewish Museum, NY / Art Resource, NY

PARTING THE WATERS
crossing the **jordan river**

A QUOTE FROM THE BIBLE
EXODUS 17:1–6

At Etham the LORD said to Moses:

"Tell the people of Israel to turn back and camp across from Pi-Hahiroth near Baal-Zephon, between Migdol and the Red Sea. The king will think they were afraid to cross the desert and that they are wandering around, trying to find another way to leave the country. I will make the king stubborn again, and he will try to catch you. Then I will destroy him and his army. People everywhere will praise me for my victory, and the Egyptians will know that I really am the LORD." The Israelites obeyed the LORD and camped where he told them.

When the king of Egypt heard that the Israelites had finally left, he and his officials changed their minds and said, "Look what we have done! We let them get away, and they will no longer be our slaves."

The king got his war chariot and army ready.

WATER IN THE DESERT

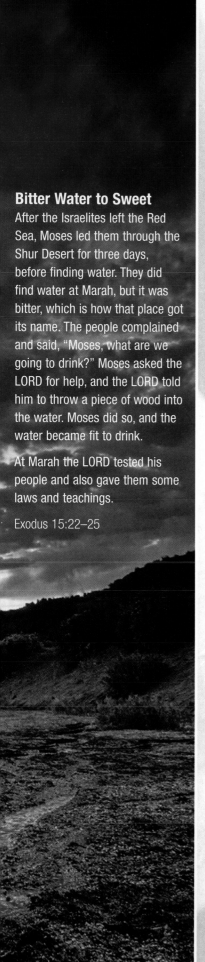

The parting of the Red Sea is the most familiar biblical account of God's mastery of water. Yet two lesser-known events, which occurred during the Israelites' long wanderings in the desert, are no less amazing.

In the first tale, God instructed Moses to throw a piece of wood into brackish water and it instantly became fit to drink. (Read Exodus 15:22–25.)

After the Israelites had journeyed a bit farther and were again in need of water, God told Moses to strike the rock at Mount Sinai with his walking stick. While the leaders of the people watched, Moses did as God had instructed him, and water poured from the rock. (Read Exodus 17:1–6.)

The Secrets of Moses and the Water

In the case of the bitter water, chemists hypothesize that Moses used the process of ion exchange, purifying the water by adding the necessary elements to alter its taste. The wood transferred ions into the water, causing it to become sweet. Jewish scholars disagree; they argue that the piece of wood Moses used was oleander *(hardufni)*, a very bitter poisonous plant. No power but God's could have transformed bitter water to sweet with bitter wood.

Physics provides one possible explanation for the waters that gushed from the rock at Moses' command. Some porous rocks, such as sandstone or limestone, act as natural underground reservoirs, gathering water in their hollow spaces. Sometimes the desert winds expose these rocks—and cover them with a crust of debris that accumulates during sandstorms, sealing the water within the stone.

Desert peoples are familiar with this unusual phenomenon, and scholars believe that in biblical times thirsty travelers sometimes broke through the rocks' gritty crust in hopes of finding water. The story of Moses and the rock might tell of just such an event. What it cannot explain is how Moses knew which rock to choose. Moses knew the answer to that: God's hand guided his.

WORKING WONDERS

In the desert spaces of the Holy Land, water is a precious substance, a metaphor for life itself. So when Jesus demonstrated his miraculous powers over water, he was demonstrating his dominion not only over nature's power but also over life's very essence. It's significant that the first miracle attributed to Jesus involved water (John 2:1–12), when he heeded his mother's call at a wedding feast in Cana and transformed common water into the finest wine—even as the Bible promises that God can transform our lives from drudgery to divine inspiration.

WITH WATER

Walking on Water

The story of Jesus walking upon the waters is one of the most compelling tales of his extraordinary powers over the laws of nature. The Bible offers three accounts of this feat, one in the Gospel written by Matthew (Read Matthew 14:22–33), one in the Gospel written by Mark (Read Mark 6:45–52), the other in the Gospel written by John (Read John 6:16–21).

In all three of these accounts, Jesus had sent his disciples on ahead of him in their boat, while he stayed behind to pray. Suddenly the seas became rough, so rough that these hardy men—most of them experienced fishermen whose lives were devoted to the sea—feared for their lives. Then, even at the storm's height, Jesus suddenly appeared through the slashing rain and wind, walking toward his disciples, his weight somehow borne aloft by the waters.

Matthew's account goes further, including a second miracle. In his telling, Peter asked Jesus if he could walk out to meet him, and Jesus told him do so. Peter stepped out of the boat and walked toward Jesus. Only when Peter looked down at the waves did he begin to sink.

Peter's brief walk atop the waves demonstrates that Jesus was no apparition, no illusion. He was there—a living, breathing man, who reached out his hand to grasp Peter and lift him back into the boat.

Calming the Sea

Jesus was not only borne aloft by water, he spoke to the sea—and it obeyed. Mark's account of Jesus' life includes the story of another storm on the Sea of Galilee, where storms still gather with sudden ferocity 2,000 years later.

Jesus, exhausted from ministering to great crowds of followers, was asleep in the boat, and his disciples were reluctant to wake him even when waves began to break over the deck and the boat and its crew were imperiled. Finally, they had no choice but to awaken him. Then they watched dumbstruck as Jesus spoke to the wind and the waves; instantly the sea calmed down and peace was restored. (Read Mark 4:35–41.)

Afterward, Jesus asked the disciples, "Why were you afraid? Don't you have any faith?" His challenge to them taught a lesson: faith is not simply an abstract virtue. Rather, faith enables. It empowers. It causes us to function differently in our world. Like a copper wire that forms an electrical connection, faith joins the natural world with the supernatural world to create a brave new world, where anything is possible and even the wind and water heed God's commands.

A QUOTE FROM THE BIBLE
JOHN 6:16–21

That evening, Jesus' disciples went down to the lake. They got into a boat and started across for Capernaum. Later that evening Jesus had still not come to them, and a strong wind was making the water rough.

When the disciples had rowed for three or four miles, they saw Jesus walking on the water. He kept coming closer to the boat, and they were terrified. But he said, "I am Jesus! Don't be afraid!" The disciples wanted to take him into the boat, but suddenly the boat reached the shore where they were headed.

In Bible days as in our own, the act of communal dining was regarded as a special occasion. And one of the great stories of Christ's miracles tells of his feeding a great multitude who had come to hear him preach— surely a reminder of the spiritual food that God offers to those who heed his call.

It is a wondrous scene: a mighty throng, thousands strong, scattered across a hillside, eager to hear the words of the Son of God. And what words he must have delivered!

The crowd's spiritual needs were certainly fulfilled. But they were only human, after all, and stomachs grew hungry as midday approached. When a boy offered to share his five loaves of bread and two fish with the crowd, Jesus blessed the meager fare, and his disciples began passing out the food … and kept passing it out … and kept passing it out. When the crowd had eaten its fill, 12 baskets of leftovers were gathered.

Here is one of the Bible's most miraculous stories, a parable of sharing and plenitude, a tale that evokes the endless bounty of God's table.

The story's importance is highlighted by a fascinating fact: all four Gospels record this remarkable scene—the only case in the New Testament when all four Gospel writers recount the same miracle.

Here is what fascinates Bible scholars about the tale:

Though this is the only miracle that each of the four Gospels recounts—(Read Matthew 14:13–21; Mark 6:30–44; Luke 9:10–17; John 6:1–15)—each account gives a slightly different picture of the scene, although the main events are unchanged.

- All four Gospels attest that the number of those who ate were about five thousand men. (Read Matthew 14:21, Mark 6:44, Luke 9:14, John 6:10.)
- Most scholars agree that the total number of people well exceeded 5,000, since each male head of household would likely have been accompanied by his wife, children, and other dependents.
- John recounts that Philip protested that it would take almost a year's wages to buy only a small amount of bread for each of those present. (Read John 6:7.)
- Some speculate that the boy's example of sharing inspired others to follow his lead, suggesting that the women in the crowd had packed some food. This theory clearly contradicts the Bible accounts.
- In all four accounts, Jesus gave thanks for five loaves and two fishes and from this small portion satisfied the hungry crowd with leftovers to spare.

God's provision was more than anyone present could imagine. Yet it still did not tax his powers.

A QUOTE FROM THE BIBLE
JOHN 6:8–14

Andrew, the brother of Simon Peter, was one of the disciples. He spoke up and said, "There is a boy here who has five small loaves of barley bread and two fish. But what good is that with all these people?" The ground was covered with grass, and Jesus told his disciples to have everyone sit down. About five thousand men were in the crowd. Jesus took the bread in his hands and gave thanks to God. Then he passed the bread to the people, and he did the same with the fish, until everyone had plenty to eat.

The people ate all they wanted, and Jesus told his disciples to gather up the leftovers, so that nothing would be wasted. The disciples gathered them up and filled twelve large baskets with what was left over from the five barley loaves.

After the people had seen Jesus work this miracle, they began saying, "This must be the Prophet who is to come into the world!"

JESUS FEEDS THE MULTITUDE

A QUOTE FROM THE BIBLE
1 KINGS 17:1–6

Elijah was a prophet from Tishbe in Gilead. One day he went to King Ahab and said, "I'm a servant of the living LORD, the God of Israel. And I swear in his name that it won't rain until I say so. There won't even be any dew on the ground." Later, the LORD said to Elijah, "Leave and go across the Jordan River so you can hide near Cherith Creek. You can drink water from the creek, and eat the food I've told the ravens to bring you."

Elijah obeyed the LORD and went to live near Cherith Creek. Ravens brought him bread and meat twice a day, and he drank water from the creek.

the prophet
ELIJAH

Elijah was God's prophet to Israel centuries before the birth of Christ. (Read 1 Kings 17–19.) He lived and prophesied during the reign of the evil King Ahab and Queen Jezebel.

Elijah's life, like that of Francis of Assisi—a Christian saint who lived centuries after him—was suffused by the supernatural, so much so that he seemed almost unfettered by the world around him, a creature of pure spirit. The tales of this child of God are miraculous indeed:

- Once when Elijah was forced to hide from Queen Jezebel because the evil woman had put a price on his head, he was fed by an angel. Throughout his time in hiding, he never hungered. After the angel left, ravens—notorious for stealing food—actually brought him food twice a day. (Read 1 Kings 19:1–9.)
- In a town called Zarephath, Elijah encountered a woman whose life was much affected by a drought. She and her son were starving. Yet Elijah asked her to feed him. The request included a promise: if she would honor him and the God he represented, her jar of flour and bottle of oil would continually be replenished for as long until [the LORD sent rain and] the drought was over. She agreed, and God honored the promise made by his prophet. (Read 1 Kings 17:8–16.)
- Supercharged by God's grace, Elijah outran the king's chariot all the way from Mount Carmel to Jezreel, almost 25 miles/about 40 kilometers. (Read 1 Kings 18:41-46.)
- When Elijah needed to cross the Jordan, he simply parted the waters—with his cloak! (Read 2 Kings 2:1–8.)
- Elijah's prayers to God also restored life to a dead boy and ended a deadly drought. (Read 1 Kings 17:17-24 and 1 Kings 18:1-2, 41-46.)

Elijah was a bearer of God's message to the Israelites. Though they had strayed from their allegiance to God and were worshiping idols—in particular the false god Baal—God wanted them back. Elijah had been entrusted with the task of calling these rebellious, but deeply loved, people back to their faith in God.

On God's behalf, Elijah challenged the prophets of Baal to a spiritual duel. Each would prepare a sacrifice and pray that his god would supply the fire to burn up those sacrifices. So confident was Elijah that he drenched his altar with water. While the opposing altar remained cold, God demonstrated his power by burning not only the wood, but the sacrifice and the altar as well. (Read 1 Kings 18:3-40.)

Elijah's was a life that didn't bear up to the usual scrutiny. And his death, like his life, defied the laws of nature: rather than die, he was carried to heaven in a chariot. It was this wondrous ascent into heaven that inspired the moving spiritual, "Swing Low, Sweet Chariot." (Read 2 Kings 2:1-18.)

A QUOTE FROM THE BIBLE
JAMES 5:16–18

The prayer of an innocent person is powerful, and it can help a lot. Elijah was just as human as we are, and for three and a half years his prayers kept the rain from falling. But when he did pray for rain, it fell from the skies and made the crops grow.

A Request is Granted

According to the Bible, Elisha's ministry lasted twice as long as Elijah's, and Elisha performed twice as many miracles as his mentor. Many scholars believe these accomplishments fulfilled Elisha's request of Elijah: "Please give me twice as much of your power as you give the other prophets, so I can be the one who takes your place as their leader" (2 Kings 2:9).

Heavy Metal?

Once, Elisha was approached by a fellow prophet who had lost a borrowed axehead in the Jordan River. Elisha cut a stick, threw it into the river, and the iron axehead floated to the surface where the worker could retrieve it. (Read 2 Kings 6:1–7.)

Iron can float when wrought into the hollow shape of a ship, but not when it is solid, like an axehead. How would a stick floating on the water prompt the metal to rise? The answer is not a matter of wood and iron, water density and gravity; it is a matter of faith.

Elisha was the prophet Elijah's successor; when Elijah ascended to heaven, Elisha picked up his mantle— the cloak with which the elder holy man had parted the Jordan River—and carried on his work. As his mentor had done before him, Elisha challenged people to return to the faith of Moses: the belief in the one true God of Abraham.

Before Elijah was taken up to heaven, Elisha prayed that he would have twice the power granted to Elijah. He did, indeed, live an exceptional life, filled with miracles and wonders.

- Elisha purified the water from the spring in the town of Jericho, and it remains fresh to this day. (Read 2 Kings 2:19–22.)
- Elisha rescued a poor widow, who was about to lose her children because of her indebtedness after the death of her husband. She had just one jar of oil, but Elisha had a miracle in mind. He sent her out to borrow as many empty jars from the townspeople as she could find. She then filled all those jars from her single small jar of oil and sold the borrowed jars of oil to pay her debts. The family continued to live off the proceeds. (Read 2 Kings 4:1–7.)
- Elisha promised a child to another woman who showed him kindness. After years of infertility, she did indeed bear a son. But a second miracle followed: when the child became sick and died, Elisha brought him back to life. (Read 2 Kings 4:8–37.)
- Elijah used flour to purify a pot of stew that had been contaminated by poisonous fruit. (Read 2 Kings 4:38-41).
- Much as Jesus later did, Elisha also multiplied several loaves of bread and sufficient grain to feed 100 people. (Read 2 Kings 4:42-44.)

On his deathbed, Elisha was visited by an admirer, Jehoash, who echoed the words Elisha himself uttered when he saw Elijah taken into heaven: "Master, what will Israel's chariots and cavalry be able to do without you?"

A QUOTE FROM THE BIBLE
2 KINGS 4:32–35

Elisha arrived at the woman's house and went straight to his room, where he saw the boy's body on his bed. He walked in, shut the door, and prayed to the LORD. Then he got on the bed and stretched out over the dead body, with his mouth on the boy's mouth, his eyes on his eyes, and his hand on his hands. As he lay there, the boy's body became warm. Elisha got up and walked back and forth in the room, then he went back and leaned over the boy's body. The boy sneezed seven times and opened his eyes.

the prophet
ELISHA

A QUOTE FROM THE BIBLE

HEBREWS 4:12

What God has said isn't only alive and active! It is sharper than any double-edged sword. His word can cut through our spirits and souls and through our joints and marrow, until it discovers the desires and thoughts of our hearts.

CHAPTER 11

the Bible
itself is a mystery

The biggest mystery of the Bible may be that it exists at all—that its ancient texts have survived down the centuries, to exert unique spiritual influence on men and women today. Unlike sacred writings such as the Koran and the Book of Mormon, the 66 books of the Holy Bible had no single person as their author. In fact, over an estimated 1,600 years, forty different authors from all walks of life—including kings, shepherds, priests, prophets, a physician, a tax collector, a leatherworker, and several fishermen—wrote the poetry, history, laws, and teachings found in the Old and New Testaments. The Bible was not even written in a single tongue: its authors employed three languages—Hebrew, Greek, and Aramaic.

Page to the right:
Page from a 14th-century Greek lectionary
(Manuscript on vellum in ABS Library)

φήτας καὶ σοφούς·
καὶ γραμματεῖς· καὶ
ἐξ αὐτῶν ἀποκτεν-
εῖτε· καὶ σταυρώσε-
τε· καὶ ἐξ αὐτῶν μα-
στιγώσετε ἐν ταῖς συνα-
γωγαῖς ὑμῶν· καὶ δι-
ώξετε ἀπὸ πόλεως
εἰς πόλιν· ὅπως ἔλ-
θῃ ἐφ' ὑμᾶς πᾶν αἷ-
μα δίκαιον ἐκχυνό-
μενον ἐπὶ τῆς γῆς·
ἀπὸ τοῦ αἵματος Ἄβελ
τοῦ δικαίου, ἕως τοῦ
αἵματος Ζαχαρίου υἱοῦ
Βαραχίου· ὃν ἐφονεύ-
σατε μεταξὺ τοῦ
ναοῦ καὶ τοῦ θυσια-
στηρίου· ἀμὴν λέγω
ὑμῖν, ὅτι ἥξει πάντα
ταῦτα, ἐπὶ τὴν γενε-
ὰν ταύτην· ἱερουσα-

λήμ· ἡ ἀποκτέν-
νουσα τοὺς προφήτας· καὶ
λιθοβολοῦσα τοὺς
ἀπεσταλμένους πρὸς
αὐτήν· ποσάκις ἠθέ-
λησα ἐπισυναγαγεῖν
τὰ τέκνα σου· ὃν τρό-
πον, ἐπισυνάγει ὄρ-
νις τὰ νοσσία ἑαυτῆς,
ὑπὸ τὰς πτέρυγας·
Καὶ οὐκ ἠθελήσατε·
ἰδοὺ ἀφίεται ὑμῖν ὁ
οἶκος ὑμῶν, ἔρημος·
λέγω γὰρ ὑμῖν, οὐ μή με
ἴδητε ἀπ' ἄρτι· ἕως ἂν
εἴπητε, εὐλογημένος
ὁ ἐρχόμενος ἐν ὀνό-
ματι κυρίου:
Ἐκ τοῦ κατὰ Ματθαῖον:
Εἶπεν ὁ κ(ύριο)ς τοῖς ἑαυτοῦ
μαθηταῖς· ὁ ὑπομεί-
νας εἰς τέλος οὗτος σω-

The word Bible is derived from the Greek word *biblia*, meaning "books."

Portions of the Bible have been translated into more than 2,400 languages—more than any other book in history—and the complete Bible is available in over 400 languages.

A QUOTE FROM THE BIBLE

2 TIMOTHY 3:16–17

Everything in the Scriptures is God's Word. All of it is useful for teaching and helping people and for correcting them and showing them how to live. The Scriptures train God's servants to do all kinds of good deeds.

**Hebrew Bible
(Old Testament in
Christian Bibles)**

Genesis
Exodus
Leviticus
Numbers
Deuteronomy
Joshua
Judges
Ruth
1 Samuel
2 Samuel
1 Kings
2 Kings
1 Chronicles
2 Chronicles
Ezra
Nehemiah
Esther
Job
Psalms
Proverbs
Ecclesiastes
Song of Songs
Isaiah
Jeremiah
Lamentations
Ezekiel
Daniel
Hosea
Joel
Amos
Obadiah
Jonah
Micah
Nahum
Habakkuk
Zephaniah
Haggai
Zechariah
Malachi

**Other books included
in the Old Testaments
of some Christian traditions***

Tobit
Judith
Esther (Greek Version)
Wisdom of Solomon
Sirach (Ecclesiasticus)
Baruch
Letter of Jeremiah
Prayer of Azariah and Song of the Three Hebrews
Susanna
Bel and the Dragon
1 Maccabees
2 Maccabees
1 Esdras
Prayer of Manasseh
Psalm 151
3 Maccabees
2 Esdras
4 Maccabees

* These books are sometimes referred to as "deuterocanonical" or "apocryphal."

the old and new testaments

The Holy Bible consists of two major sections, the Old and the New Testaments. Three major world religions trace their roots to the ancient Hebrew Scriptures widely called the Old Testament.

To Muslims the Old Testament is a revered but tainted historical source. To Jews it is the God-given Tanakh, or Hebrew Bible, comprised of three main sections: the Law, the Prophets, and the Writings. To Christians, the Old Testament is the sacred beginning of God's revelation, the history of the chosen people who look forward to the promised Messiah.

The first five books of the Bible, or the Torah, trace their beginnings to the ministry of one of Israel's early leaders, Moses. Parts of these books may have been passed on by word of mouth, with little change, from as early as 1400 BC! The last prophet of the Old Testament, Malachi, recorded his message in the fifth century BC. Thus, over an astounding ten centuries, prophets, kings, court historians, shepherds, and the tribal leaders called judges captured the dramatic story of the chosen people, the Israelites, and their revelations and teachings about their one true God.

The New Testament was written in a comparatively short period of time after Jesus Christ's life on earth—from AD 50 to around AD 125. It is Christianity's account of the birth, life, death, and resurrection of Jesus and the creation of the church he founded. The New Testament also contains teachings on how to live as a Christian, one who follows Christ.

Somehow, though stretched over centuries and expressed through many different writers, there is one universal message conveyed in the Bible from its first book, Genesis, to its last, Revelation: the Creator loves his creatures and has provided a way for them to know him and be one with him. The Bible is a road map for that spiritual journey.

preserving the writings

Without the anonymous scribes of old, we would have no Genesis, no Revelation—nor anything in between. Through thousands of years, scribes preserved the original words of the sacred texts, a miracle in itself.

Both Jewish and Christian scribes approached their exacting task as a sacred mission, for they were guarding the very message of God. Century by century they meticulously recorded every letter of Scripture onto the paper-like papyrus made of dried reeds, or onto the thin leather material called parchment. The original sources they relied upon may have been lost, but the copies were amazingly preserved, thanks to the diligence of these devoted men and women.

When you review the facts, it's surprising that skeptics question the authenticity of the Bible. Scholars accept the writings of ancient individuals such as Aristotle or Virgil based on just a handful of documents. Yet by contrast, there are in many cases thousands of surviving copies of the texts that make up the Bible.

A famous example is the Dead Sea Scrolls. Shortly after World War II, shepherds and archaeologists discovered ancient jars in eleven caves near Qumran on the Dead Sea in what is now Israel. Hidden like time capsules for nearly two thousand years, the jars contained thousands of fragments representing between 825 and 870 writings. Portions of every book of the Old Testament except Esther were discovered. Some of these scrolls had circulated during the second century BC and the first century AD, making them centuries older than the best manuscripts that scholars had available to them up to that time.

These significant translations and texts below are the primary sources of our modern versions of the Bible.

The Judean Wilderness

The Dead Sea Caves

The Septuagint
The Old Testament was translated into Greek during the three centuries before Christ. "Septuagint" refers to the number 70; it was so named because it was believed that 72 Jewish scholars translated the Scriptures for the Egyptian Pharaoh Ptolemy II.

The Masoretic Text
Named for the Masoretes, the most influential group of Hebrew scribes, this text is the foundation for most modern translations of the Hebrew Bible. The oldest Masoretic manuscripts date from the 9th century AD.

The Aleppo Codex
Dated from the 10th century AD, this exquisite manuscript was possibly the first complete copy of the Masoretic Text. Written in Jerusalem and Tiberias, it was taken to Aleppo, Syria, in the 14th century, where it remained until it was returned, incomplete, to Israel in 1958.

The Vulgate
Saint Jerome's 4th century AD translation of the Bible into Latin remains a standard text in the Roman Catholic Church and is an important tool for helping scholars understand difficult passages in Hebrew and Greek texts.

A QUOTE FROM THE BIBLE
2 PETER 1:20–21

You need to realize that no one alone can understand any of the prophecies in the Scriptures. The prophets did not think these things up on their own, but they were guided by the Spirit of God.

Image on right page: Scroll of Isaiah. From one of the Dead Sea Scrolls.

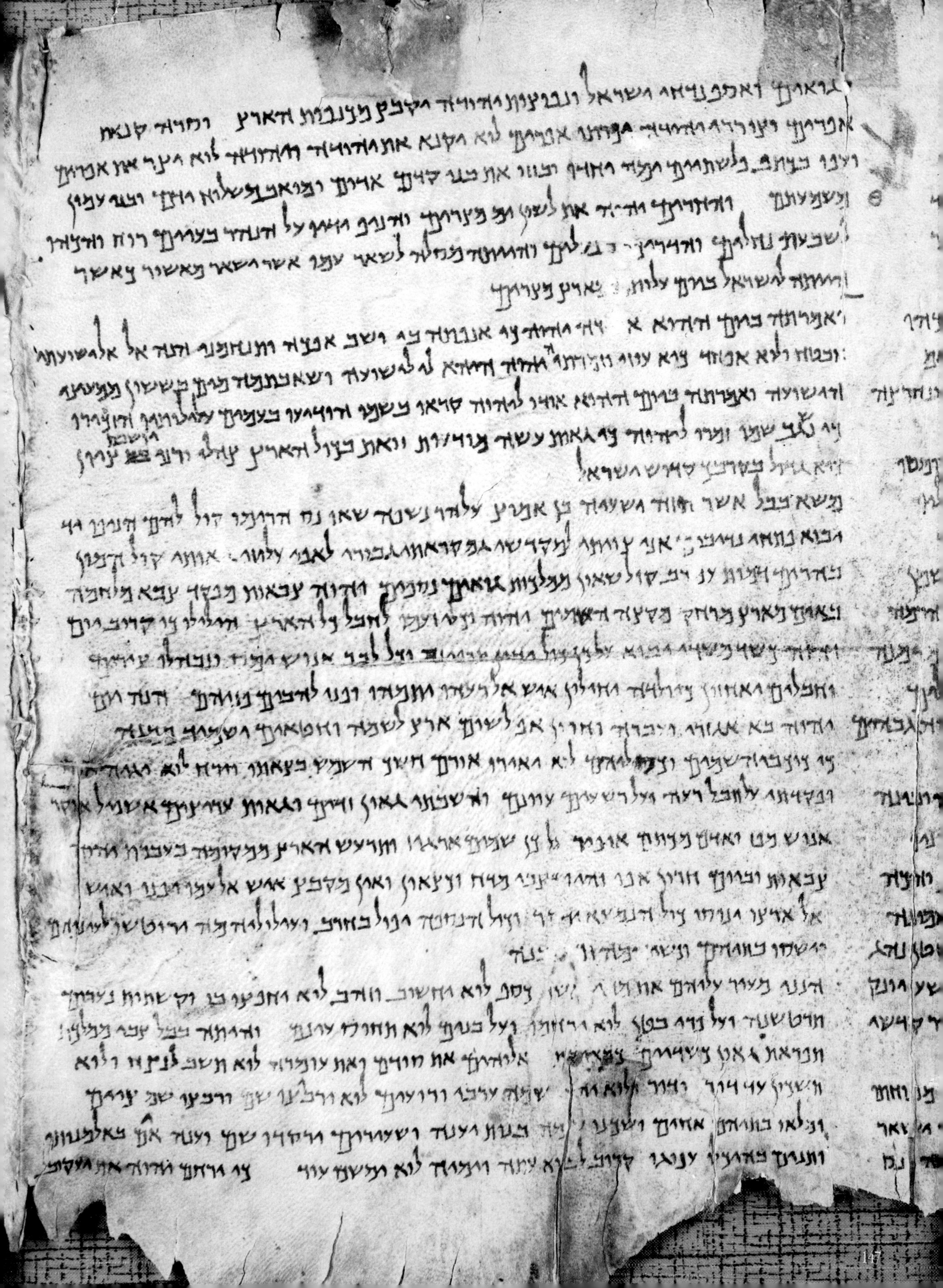

fighting words?

The Bible's message of love and freedom is both challenging and revolutionary: so much so that over the centuries wars have been fought because of it.

The movement to put Scripture into the everyday language of the people cost countless martyrs their lives. This is difficult to understand today—not only are there hundreds of translations but hundreds of versions as well, including special editions designed for specific groups: sport coaches, business people, new brides, and retirees, to name only a few. There are even Bibles printed like magazines.

The first book inventor Johann Gutenberg created on his revolutionary printing press in 1455 was the Bible in. But its text was in Latin, and common people couldn't read it. The Roman Catholic church kept a tight rein on Scripture, persecuting early translators like John Wycliffe (d. 1384) and William Tyndale (d. 1536), who believed that all Christians should have access to God's Word and be allowed to interpret it themselves.

Eventually the King James Version, published in 1611, became the translation used by English-speaking Protestants. The Douay-Rheims predated the King James Version by a few years and was favored by Roman Catholics for the next four hundred years.

Johann Gutenberg invented the printing press in the mid-15th century AD.

Who decided what was included in the Holy Bible?

That's an important question, considering that hundreds of religious writings from antiquity—such as the *Gospel of Judas* first published in 2006—were not included. The answer, however, is not as mysterious as it might seem. The structure and books of the Old Testament were settled five hundred years before Christ. For writings to be included in the New Testament, they had to be either written by an apostle or someone closely linked to the first generation of church leaders, and they had to be in continuous use by churches as well. The books that now make up the New Testament were already generally accepted when, in AD 367, church father Athanasius drew up his famous list of what we call the canon of Scripture.

Do all Bibles have the same books?

Roman Catholic and Orthodox Bibles include several Jewish writings that were preserved only in Greek rather than Hebrew versions. These include historical books like 1 & 2 Maccabees, dramatic stories like Tobit, Judith, and Susanna, and writings of great wisdom like Sirach.

Why wasn't the *Gospel of Judas* included?

The *Gospel of Judas* was widely publicized through books and documentaries produced by the National Geographic Society after its publication in 2006.

While Judas is not claimed as the writer of this gospel, this writing does focus on him as a main character. In it, a "good" Judas is not Christ's betrayer but his liberator, commissioned to "sacrifice the man that clothes" Jesus. This is a classic view of the 1st-century Gnostic sects that considered anything in the physical realm tainted. This set of beliefs was considered a heresy by the early church leaders who had known Jesus and those who were mentored by Jesus' disciples. While it is likely that some of the early church leaders knew the *Gospel of Judas*, it was not considered as authoritative as the other writings that were included in the Bible. Based on this, the early church intentionally omitted this book from the New Testament.

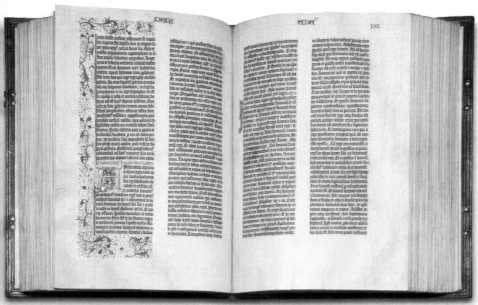

Johann Gutenberg (c. 1390/1400–c.1468)
Biblia Latina. Mainz: Johann Gutenberg & Johann Fust (c.1455).

When the Bible was first mass-produced in the age of the printing press, there were some versions that came to be known by the glaring typos, or spelling errors, that marred their pages.

The Ears to Ear Bible (1810): Matthew 13:43 reads, "Who hath ears to ear, let him hear."

The Fool Bible: Printed for Charles I, its Psalm 14:1 reads, "The fool hath said in his heart there is a God" [instead of "no God"].

The Judas Bible (1611): Matthew 26:36 states that "Judas" instead of "Jesus" went to Gethsemane with his disciples.

The Unrighteous Bible: A 1653 King James Version leaves out the word "not" in 1 Corinthians 6:9, "The unrighteous shall inherit the kingdom of God."*

*(From *The Christian Writer's Manual of Style*, Robert Hudson, ed. (Grand Rapids, MI: Zondervan, 2004), pp.87–88. And www.frivolity.com/teatime/Miscellaneous/and_the_word_had_a_typo.txt).

CHAPTER 12 IMPOSSIBLE

"The fastest runners and the greatest heroes don't always win races and battles," declared the author of Ecclesiastes, one of the Old Testament wisdom writings (Ecclesiastes 9:11). Indeed, the Old Testament is filled with accounts of battles in which a decided underdog pulls off an upset victory using a unique and unconventional strategy—what you might

MISSIONS

call a "sacred strategy." For Old Testament heroes viewed politics, war, and religion as different facets of the same struggle, God's struggle. Their loyalty to their God—and his loyalty to them—made for an unbeatable combination. When they followed God's plan, he marched in their ranks and fought alongside them, guaranteeing their victory. Small wonder the Israelites turned to prayer not as a plea, but rather as the most potent of weapons: praising God, they set up altars amid their arsenals.

THE BATTLES OF JOSHUA

Joshua was the Patton of the Israelites: no other leader of the Hebrews created more unexpected or grandiose battle strategies than the man Moses chose to be his successor. Even when we first meet Joshua, he is seen in the midst of battle, soon after the Amalekites attacked the Hebrews at Rephidim. Exodus 17:8–16 says that Joshua pursued the enemy's forces into the valley while Moses stood on the hillside holding up his staff—the one filled with the power of God that Moses used to part the Red Sea and escape the Egyptians.

As long as the elderly Moses was able to hold his mighty staff aloft, Joshua and his men prevailed in the conflict. But each time Moses' arms grew tired and the staff was lowered, the emboldened Amalekites came roaring back to rout the Israelites. Moses' comrades Aaron and Hur, who stood with him on the hilltop overlooking the battleground, quickly grasped the situation: seating their leader on a rock, they held his arms aloft until Joshua secured the victory, just as the sun set.

After Moses' death, Joshua led the people into battle many times, as they sought to conquer the land God had promised them. Joshua's first obstacle was to capture the well-fortified city of Jericho. A heavenly messenger delivered the battle plan: the Israelites were to march around the city once a day for six days. On the seventh day, they were to march around the city seven times, sound their trumpets of war, then raise their voices in a mighty clamor. Bizarre as this sonic strategy must have sounded, Joshua did exactly as the messenger had instructed, until, as the old song tells us, the walls came tumblin' down. (Find the story in Joshua 6.)

In another phenomenal event, the Israelites were pressing hard against a coalition of enemy armies, but were quickly losing daylight. Soon their enemies would be able to escape into the darkness. Joshua looked skyward and said: "Our LORD, make the sun stop in the sky over Gibeon, and the moon stand still over Aijalon Valley" (Joshua 10:12). In response to his prayer, we are told, "the sun stood still and didn't go down for about a whole day" (Joshua 10:13). As if to emphasize the weight of that statement, the next verse says: "Never before and never since has the LORD done anything like that for someone who prayed."

What, exactly, happened that day? Did the earth literally stop spinning on its axis? Had that happened, the sudden cessation of rotation would have sent everyone and everything flying across the earth's surface with great force. Some people think that light may have been refracted to Joshua's location from other places, keeping it illuminated. Others suggest that the sun simply didn't burn as hotly or brightly throughout the day, allowing the soldiers to continue fighting when they otherwise would be taking a break. Any logical explanation requires much conjecture.

On another day, Joshua and his forces did battle to vanquish the city of Ai (pronounced AY-eye). But this conflict was significant for a different reason: though Ai was considerably smaller and less imposing than Jericho, the Israelites were soundly defeated, a sign of the LORD's displeasure over the sin of Achan, who was guilty of looting Jericho after its fall, against God's clear command. Here was a telling message from on high: one person's failings can have a devastating effect on the lives of others. (Read Joshua 7 for the full details of this story.)

A QUOTE FROM THE BIBLE
JOSHUA 6:2–5

The LORD said to Joshua:

With my help, you and your army will defeat the king of Jericho and his army, and you will capture the town. Here is how to do it: March slowly around Jericho once a day for six days. Take along the sacred chest and have seven priests walk in front of it, carrying trumpets. But on the seventh day, march slowly around the town seven times while the priests blow their trumpets. Then the priests will blast on their trumpets, and everyone else will shout. The wall will fall down, and your soldiers can go straight in from every side.

The oasis of Jericho in Israel blooms against the surrounding desert. The horns of Jericho were sounded during Joshua's conquest (Joshua 2:1).

Gideon's first battle was a spiritual one: God ordered him to tear down a nearby altar to the Canaanite god Baal. Still unsure of his power and his calling, Gideon performed the task at night to avoid being seen. Yet he was soon found out. When the townspeople discovered what he had done, they cried out: "kill him!" Gideon's father rescued him only after diplomatically suggesting that if Baal had been a real god, he would certainly have avenged himself against Gideon.

God next instructed Gideon to take a stand against the powerful Midianites, who were tormenting Israel. So anxious was he about the assignment that he asked God to confirm his word through a sign. Gideon placed a fleece on the ground one night, asking that in the morning it would be wet with dew, even though the ground was dry. It happened exactly as he asked. Still Gideon was reluctant; he requested an additional sign. This time, he asked that in the morning the ground would be wet while the fleece was dry. Again, it happened just as he had requested.

Finally convinced that he had earned God's support, Gideon prepared to face the Midianites with a mighty army of 32,000 men. But now God unveiled a truly unconventional strategy, one designed to show the people that their strength must be rooted in their faith, not their numbers. God instructed Gideon to release any men who were afraid to go into battle. Two of every three men—22,000 soldiers in all—immediately departed. Then Gideon was told to lead the remaining men to the water's edge and watch them drink. Only those who knelt and drank by putting their faces in the water were asked to stay.

After this further reduction in its ranks, Gideon's "army" consisted of a squad of only some 300 soldiers. The warriors were divided into three groups of 100 and positioned around the enemy's camp—armed, not with swords, but with trumpets in their right hands and torches covered by clay jars in their left. At Gideon's signal, the men blew their trumpets and smashed the jars. The surprise attack worked brilliantly: the sudden bright lights and overwhelming noise panicked the enemy soldiers; they drew their swords and began to fight one another as they fled into the darkness. The Israelites pursued them and prevailed. Gideon, the unlikely hero, had indeed proved himself to be a "strong warrior."

A QUOTE FROM THE BIBLE
JUDGES 6:11–14

One day an angel from the LORD went to the town of Ophrah and sat down under the big tree that belonged to Joash, a member of the Abiezer clan. Joash's son Gideon was nearby, threshing grain in a shallow pit, where he could not be seen by the Midianites...

Then the LORD himself said, "Gideon, you will be strong, because I am giving you the power to rescue Israel from the Midianites."

This cave near today's Ein Harod, Israel, is near the site where God reduced the size of Gideon's army before the battle against the Midianites. Only those men who knelt down and lapped up the water from the source were chosen for the battle (Read Judges 7:5-6).

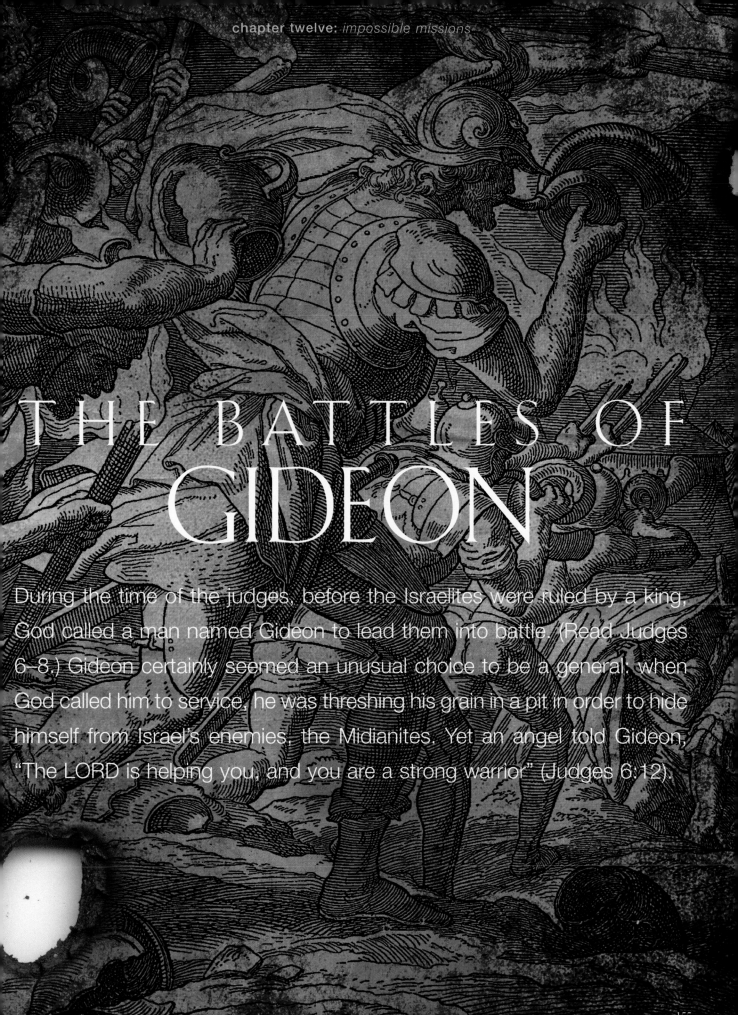

THE BATTLES OF GIDEON

During the time of the judges, before the Israelites were ruled by a king, God called a man named Gideon to lead them into battle. (Read Judges 6–8.) Gideon certainly seemed an unusual choice to be a general: when God called him to service, he was threshing his grain in a pit in order to hide himself from Israel's enemies, the Midianites. Yet an angel told Gideon, "The LORD is helping you, and you are a strong warrior" (Judges 6:12).

THE BATTLES OF
SAMSON

The Israelites' long-awaited occupation of the promised land of Canaan did not always go smoothly. They prospered at times, but the power of their armies always reflected the power of their faith, and when their love of God diminished, they often fell under the sway of their enemies. In one such period, the Israelites had been ruled by the Philistines, an aggressive people, for more than forty years when an angel of the Lord announced to Samson's parents that, despite their previous inability to conceive a child, they would now give birth to a son. (Read Judges 13:2–5.)

Samson's parents were told that their son was to be raised as a Nazirite, an ascetic sect of the Israelites. As such, he would take an ancient vow of intense spiritual dedication. As a symbol of his commitment to the ways of the Nazirites, Samson would never cut his hair. His long, flowing locks would be a sign that the boy had been set apart by God for a great purpose.

While the Philistines ruled Israel with a stern hand, Samson, nourished by God's grace, grew in strength—and kept growing. He became amazingly strong, frustrating the Philistines' attempts to control him. Once, having been mistreated by his Philistine father-in-law, Samson found revenge by catching 300 foxes, pairing them up, and tying torches to their tails. Then he set the foxes free to run through the Philistines' fields, burning their crops to the ground. When the Philistines sent men to retaliate, Samson killed 1,000 of them with, of all things, the jawbone of a donkey. Then, tired and thirsty from the battle, he called out to God—and a mysterious stream of water came rushing from the ground. (Read Judges 15:1–20.) Samson seemed unstoppable.

The Philistines could not hope to outfight Samson, nor could they discover the mysterious source of his great strength, his long hair and the vow it represented. Finally, the Philistines offered the infamous temptress Delilah 1,100 pieces of silver if she could discover Samson's secret. The moment Samson revealed to Delilah that his parents had taken a vow never to cut his hair, she knew his weakness. While Samson slept, the Philistine woman clipped one long-flowing lock after another from his head, until his hair —and his strength—were gone. Samson awoke to find himself surrounded and helpless for the first time in his life. The vengeful Philistines put out his eyes, blinding the strong man, and put him to work in their mills.

Samson's enemies seemed to take little notice as his hair grew and his strength returned. When they paraded their captive in front of an enormous crowd in their temple, Samson took his revenge: he pushed against the building's pillars until they fell and the temple collapsed, burying both Samson and his enemies. In this single suicidal deed, Samson killed more Philistines in the act of his death than he had killed during his lifetime. Samson's captors had solved the mystery of his great strength, but they had overlooked its true source: his vow to serve God. (Read all about Samson in Judges, chapters 13–16.)

A QUOTE FROM THE BIBLE
JUDGES 16:28–30

Samson prayed, "Please remember me, LORD God. The Philistines poked out my eyes, but make me strong one last time, so I can take revenge for at least one of my eyes!"

Samson was standing between the two middle columns that held up the roof [of the Philistine temple]. He felt around and found one column with his right hand, and the other with his left hand.

Then he shouted, "Let me die with the Philistines!" He pushed against the columns as hard as he could, and the temple collapsed with the Philistine rulers and everyone else still inside. Samson killed more Philistines when he died than he had killed during his entire life.

Samson fought the Philistines near these hills between Beit Shemesh and Jerusalem (Judges 15:16).

The hidden reality was that God had already anointed David as Israel's next king. The prophet Samuel, a national leader of the day, had privately sought out David's family and declared him as God's choice for the office. (Read 1 Samuel 16:1–13.) Despite this, David deeply believed he should let God decide when he would actually assume the throne. Until then, David remained loyal to King Saul.

In the meantime, the jealous Saul ordered David's assassination. Catching wind of the plot, the young warrior slipped away to the wilderness, where he formed a small ragtag army and waited, a future king in hiding. Staying out of sight, he moved from cave to cave with his band of guerrillas. Saul was unnerved to discover that David had twice doubled back on him, penetrated his camp and stood close enough to kill him—yet hadn't done so. (Read 1 Samuel 26.)

David was a clever, creative strategist. Often, while avoiding Saul's soldiers, he cunningly sought refuge where least expected: in the ranks of Israel's greatest enemy, the Philistines. He once tricked the Philistine king into believing that he was fighting and looting the Israelites, when he was in fact waging war against the king's own settlements! During this time, David's survival depended on his ability to convince the Philistines that they might enlist his help against Israel, while seeing to it that he never raised a hand against his homeland. (Read 1 Samuel 27.)

It was a double life, a life of disguise, deceit, and subterfuge. But David, sustained by his close relationship with God, was up to the task. That relationship is celebrated in the Psalms, many of which David wrote himself. "David my servant, is the one I chose to be king, and I will always be there to help and strengthen him . . . He will say to me 'You are my Father and my God, as well as the mighty rock where I am safe.' " (Psalm 89:20–21, 26.)

David's Mighty Men

When David became king, his ragtag army grew into a great military force. Some of the elite soldiers in his company, nicknamed "the mighty men," became legendary for their amazing exploits. In one case, a few soldiers killed hundreds of Philistines in a single encounter. In another, a single mighty man killed two of the enemy's best soldiers—and a lion in a pit for good measure. The mighty men's loyalty to David was intense. When the king craved a drink from a beloved well in his hometown of Bethlehem, three of his men broke through enemy lines and returned, their jugs brimming with water. (Read 2 Samuel 21–23.)

A QUOTE FROM THE BIBLE
2 SAMUEL 22:1–4

David sang a song to the LORD after the LORD had rescued him from his enemies, especially Saul. These are the words to David's song, or psalm:
Our LORD and our God,
you are my mighty rock,
  my fortress, my protector.
You are the rock
  where I am safe.
You are my shield,
my powerful weapon,
  and my place of shelter.
You rescue me and keep me
  from being hurt.
I praise you, our LORD!
  I prayed to you,
and you rescued me
  from my enemies.

This spring in the Cave of Ein-Gedi waters the region that descends to the Red Sea. Here David hid from a vengeful King Saul.

THE BATTLES OF
DAVID

David is one of the Old Testament's renowned heroes, a humble shepherd become one of Israel's greatest kings. Joshua and Gideon commanded entire armies, while David was more a guerrilla fighter, leading a small band of warriors who hid from the enemy, only to strike unexpectedly in small, deadly skirmishes. David's first conflict is one of the Bible's most memorable combats: as the armies of the Israelites and Philistines looked on, the shepherd boy slew the enemy's champion, the giant Goliath, with a single stone from his slingshot. This triumph was followed by a skillful skein of victories that inspired the chant: "Saul [Israel's current king] has killed a thousand enemies; David has killed ten thousand enemies!" Hearing this, King Saul became intensely jealous of David. (Read 1 Samuel 18:7–8.)

LIFE, DEATH,

CHAPTER

13

Hippocrates of Kos (often identified with Chrysippos).
Marble bust. Height 36 cm. MA 326.
Louvre, Paris, France

AND HEALING

Birth—and survival. Taken for granted today, these two events did not always walk hand in hand. Indeed, they were hard-won accomplishments in the ancient world, where infant mortality rates were staggering by the standards of the modern, industrial nations. It wasn't until 420 BC that the Greek physician Hippocrates suggested that diseases had natural causes that could be explored and treated—perhaps even cured. His belief, and the Hippocratic Oath that sprung from it—still taken by doctors today—marked the birth of medicine as we know it.

Men and women of Bible times regarded good health as a mystery rather than a science, a matter of fate utterly out of their control. But those who knew and loved God did have a Creator to whom they could plead their case. And they were not disappointed. The Bible is filled with accounts of God's intervening in the lives of humans, often bringing new life—suddenly, memorably, and inexplicably—out of infertility, sickness, even death.

The following pages recall just a few of these marvelous stories. Though the causes of the diseases and disabilities that plagued biblical figures may no longer be a mystery to us today, the presence of God in these stories of healing still commands our awe. And the Bible's accounts of the dead returning to life offer hope for all of us who, like the psalmist of the Old Testament, must one day walk through valleys as dark as death.

An estimated 5.3 million American couples know firsthand how debilitating, depressing, and stressful infertility can be. The inability to become pregnant can stalk your thoughts, sap your energy, devour your finances, and strain your relationship. Still, couples today are fortunate: they have an impressive array of options at their disposal to aid in fertility, including prescription drugs that increase and regulate ovulation, corrective surgery, even *in vitro* fertilization.

In the ancient world, there were no human answers for infertility, which carried much more cultural significance to the ancients than it does to us. To people of that time, bearing children was a sign of God's favor. Conversely, barrenness sent an unsettling message to the community: surely the failure to conceive was a sign of God's displeasure. What sin had been committed to cause such punishment? A woman's barrenness not only invited whispers and raised eyebrows, it also involved profound social adjustments: it meant the end of the family line and ensured there were no heirs to which land could be passed.

Women of the Bible like Sarah, Rebecca, Hannah, and Elizabeth sought help through prayer—and then waited for their miracle.

- Sarah was well past her childbearing years when God promised her husband Abraham that they would conceive a son. Despite the seemingly insurmountable natural odds, God's promise came to pass. At the age of 90, Sarah gave birth to Isaac (Genesis 18:1-15; Genesis 21:1-8).
- Isaac and his wife also had difficulty conceiving. The Bible says that some years into their marriage, "Rebekah still had no children. So Isaac asked the LORD to let her have a child, and the LORD answered his prayer" (Genesis 25:21). The result of that pregnancy was twin boys: Jacob and Esau. Jacob became the father of twelve sons and one daughter and the patriarch of the tribes of Israel.
- Later in Israel's history, years of infertility drove a woman named Hannah into the temple, where she poured out her heart to God. After observing her grief and talking with her, Eli the priest said, "You may go home now and stop worrying. I'm sure the God of Israel will answer your prayer" (1 Samuel 1:17). Hannah conceived and bore a son, Samuel, whose name means "God heard." He became a great prophet of God and anointed the first two kings of Israel's monarchy.
- In the New Testament, Elizabeth, the cousin of Mary, conceived her son, John, after God heard her husband's prayers for a child. The Bible tells us this birth happened when "both Zechariah and Elizabeth were already old" (Luke 1:7).

Basal thermometers? Laparoscopes? All the tools of modern medicine might not have helped these women. But God heard their pleas—and answered.

A QUOTE FROM THE BIBLE
1 SAMUEL 1:10–12

Hannah was brokenhearted and was crying as she prayed, "LORD All-Powerful, I am your servant, but I am so miserable! Please let me have a son. I will give him to you for as long as he lives, and his hair will never be cut." Hannah prayed silently to the LORD for a long time.

UNEXPECTING

A QUOTE FROM THE BIBLE

LUKE 1:28–31, 34–37

The angel greeted Mary and said, "You are truly blessed! The Lord is with you."

Mary was confused by the angel's words and wondered what they meant. Then the angel told Mary, "Don't be afraid! God is pleased with you, and you will have a son. His name will be Jesus." …

Mary asked the angel, "How can this happen? I am not married!" The angel answered, "The Holy Spirit will come down to you, and God's power will come over you. So your child will be called the holy Son of God. Your relative Elizabeth is also going to have a son, even though she is old. No one thought she could ever have a baby, but in three months she will have a son. Nothing is impossible for God!"

A 14th-century icon on display in a church in a mountain village in Crete, Greece.

AMAZING

Pregnancy, life renewing life, is always a miraculous occurrence. But it is never more miraculous than when it fulfills prophecy.

Rebekah, the wife of Isaac, finally conceived twins after her husband prayed and asked God to heal her infertility. But during her pregnancy, she felt her unborn children struggling within her. Worried that something was wrong, she prayed. God answered with these words: "Your two sons will become two separate nations. The younger of the two will be stronger, and the older son will be his servant." (Genesis 25:23)

And that's exactly what happened. Though they were twins, the boys grew to be men of greatly differing personalities and temperaments. Esau, the elder, was a hunter, while Jacob, the younger, preferred to stay near the tents. The Bible recounts their story this way: One evening, Esau returned from his hunting with a raging appetite, noted that Jacob had made a lentil stew, and begged his brother for a bowl. Jacob offered him a deal: give me your birthright and the stew is yours. Esau agreed, ate the stew, and promptly forgot the incident. But Jacob did not. With his mother's help, he donned the rough hide of a goat, tricked his aging father, and received both the blessing and the birthright due Esau. The prophecy given to Rebekah was fulfilled (Genesis 25:27-34; Genesis 27:1-40).

PREGNANCIES

The Bible doesn't reveal Mary's exact age when she conceived Jesus, but scholars agree she quite young. The Scripture reads: "This is how Jesus Christ was born. A young woman Mary was engaged to Joseph from King David's family. But before they were married, that she was going to have a baby by God's Holy Spirit" (Matthew 1:18).

When Joseph learned of the pregnancy, he came to a natural, entirely understan Mary had been with another man. But God sent an angel to speak to Joseph in confirming that the child Mary was carrying had, indeed, been conceived by The Gospel writer, Matthew, understood the circumstances surrounding Jes the words recorded 700 years earlier in Isaiah 7:14 and wrote: So the Lo came true, just as the prophet had said, "A virgin will have a baby boy, and he wi manuel," which means "God is with us." (Matthew 18:22, 23)

For centuries, leprosy haunted people of all ages and backgrounds with visions of inflamed, diseased skin and mutilated limbs. The infectious disease not only attacked one's body, but also one's place in the community. Disfigured and banished from society, lepers often lived as outcasts, shunned and feared by their neighbors.

Today we know that leprosy, now often called Hansen's Disease, is caused by an infectious bacillus, *Mycobacterium leprae*. The disease invades the skin, the nerves, the sinuses, the eyes. If left untreated, it will eventually invade even the internal organs.

Fortunately, modern medicine can cure leprosy with simple antibiotics. In 2005 the World Health Organization reported a dramatic, worldwide decline in leprosy for two consecutive years. Instances dropped 21 percent from 2003 to 2004 and 38 percent from 2004 to 2005.

This remarkable progress was made possible by an aggressive campaign that sent health workers into remote communities in such hard-hit nations as India, Nepal, Myanmar, Brazil, Madagascar and Mozambique, where they established educational services and employed new multi-drug therapies for the afflicted. Medical professionals now believe it may soon be possible to make this most dreaded disease of ancient history … well, ancient history.

The original Hebrew word for leprosy in the Bible is Tzara'ath, which literally means a "smiting" or a "stroke." The early Hebrews believed it was a punishment from God for certain acts. There was no cure. A person who contracted leprosy could look forward to a life of disfigurement, isolation, and eventual death. Lepers were required to live outside the camp or city (read Numbers 5:1–4; 12:9–15), and had to cry "I'm unclean! I'm unclean!" in warning to anyone who approached. (Read Leviticus 13:45.)

In the New Testament, Jesus healed lepers on a number of occasions, showing compassion for these suffering outcasts, while demonstrating his divine ability to heal. (Read Matthew 8:2–3; Mark 1:40–42.)

The word Tzara'ath also referred to a spreading growth found on bags, clothing, bricks, and walls of homes. (Read Leviticus 13:47–59; 14:37–48.) Could this refer to a toxic mold? In fact, biblical leprosy was more closely connected to the idea of uncleanness than disease. This may explain why the book of Leviticus includes instructions for dealing with mere mildew. The priests were responsible for inspecting suspicious spots on skin, homes, and belongings.

Who was healed of leprosy in the Bible?

- Miriam, sister to Moses and Aaron, was afflicted and then cleansed of leprosy. (Read Numbers 12:1–14.)
- Naaman, commander of the Syrian army, was cleansed of leprosy. (Read 2 Kings 5:1–19.)
- Gehazi, Elisha's once trusted servant, whose duplicity brought on the disease. (Read 2 Kings 5:20–27.)
- Uzziah, King of Judah, was struck with leprosy after he wantonly entered the temple and offered incense in spite of the high priest's objections. (Read 2 Chronicles 26:19–21.)
- Jesus cleansed ten lepers, yet only one returned to thank him. (Read Luke 17:11–19.)
- Jesus cleansed one lonely leper. (Read Matthew 8:1–4; Mark 1:40–45; Luke 5:12–16.)

"UNCLEAN!"

A QUOTE FROM THE BIBLE
LUKE 17:11–19

On his way to Jerusalem, Jesus went along the border between Samaria and Galilee. As he was going into a village, ten men with leprosy came toward him. They stood at a distance and shouted, "Jesus, Master, have pity on us!"

Jesus looked at them and said, "Go show yourselves to the priests." On their way they were healed. When one of them discovered that he was healed, he came back, shouting praises to God. He bowed down at the feet of Jesus and thanked him. The man was from the country of Samaria.

Jesus asked, "Weren't ten men healed? Where are the other nine? Why was this foreigner the only one who came back to thank God?" Then Jesus told the man, "You may get up and go. Your faith has made you well."

Who was raised from the dead?

As amazing as it may seem, the Bible tells us there were a number of individuals, not only Jesus and Lazarus, who were restored to life after their deaths.

- The widow's son, resurrected by the prophet Elijah. (Read 1 Kings 17:17–24.)

- The Shunammite woman's son, resurrected by the prophet Elisha. (Read 2 Kings 4:8–37.)

- A man whose dead body touched Elisha's bones in the grave. (Read 2 Kings 13:21.)

- Jairus' daughter, resurrected by Jesus. (Read Luke 8:40–56.)

- The widow of Nain's son, resurrected by Jesus. (Read Luke 7:11–17.)

- Lazarus, resurrected by Jesus' verbal command. (Read John 11:1–44.)

- A number of dead people or 'holy saints' were also resurrected on the day Jesus overcame death. (Read Matthew 27:51–53.)

- Jesus himself, who appeared after his resurrection in a "glorified body." (Read Matthew 28:1–10; Mark 16:1–18; Luke 24:1–8; Luke 24:13–35; John 20:1–29; John 21:1–14.)

- Tabitha, known as Dorcas, resurrected by Peter. (Read Acts 9:36–43.)

- Eutychus, resurrected by Paul after he fell out of a third story window. (Read Acts 20:7–12.)

Modern doctors can peer into our bodies and brains, even decipher our genetic code. But they can't bring the dead back to life.

Master illusionists can thrill us with their seeming mastery of natural forces. But they can't bring the dead back to life.

Great preachers can move us with their words, evoking fear and inspiring wonder. But they can't bring the dead back to life.

Charismatic musicians can rouse our spirits and unite vast crowds into a single, pulsating organism. But they can't bring the dead back to life.

The Bible, however, recounts a number of occasions when the dead were brought back to life. Were these mere illusions? Or mass hallucinations? Perhaps these individuals weren't really dead at all. Is it possible that they were near death, in some type of coma? Consider these facts:

- Lazarus had been dead and buried for four days.
- Jesus spent two days in the tomb before rising from the dead on the third.
- Even if Jesus had been able to recover from the excruciating punishment of the crucifixion— it's unlikely that anyone has ever survived such treatment—the Bible states that a soldier, in the customary Roman way, pierced Jesus' side with a spear to ensure that he was dead.
- After his resurrection, Jesus was seen by more than 500 people throughout the forty days prior to his ascension into heaven (1 Corinthians 15:6). As for the historical record, the first four books of the New Testament (Matthew, Mark, Luke, John) record eyewitness accounts that had been passed on by those who knew Jesus personally.

As difficult as it is to comprehend a resurrection, Jesus apparently rose from the dead. And the Bible records quite a few other resurrections. After all, if God has dominion over the laws of nature, then he is equally the master of the laws of death and life.

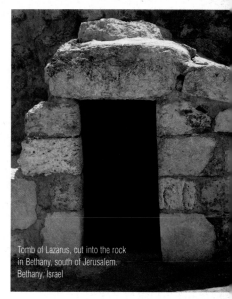

Tomb of Lazarus, cut into the rock in Bethany, south of Jerusalem. Bethany, Israel

A QUOTE FROM THE BIBLE

JOHN 11:38-40, 43-44

Jesus was still terribly upset. So he went to the tomb, which was a cave with a stone rolled against the entrance. Then he told the people to roll the stone away. But Martha said, "Lord, you know that Lazarus has been dead four days, and there will be a bad smell."

Jesus replied, "Didn't I tell you that if you had faith, you would see the glory of God?"

When Jesus had finished praying, he shouted, "Lazarus, come out!" The man who had been dead came out. His hands and feet were wrapped with strips of burial cloth, and a cloth covered his face.

Jesus then told the people, "Untie him and let him go."

UP FROM THE DEAD

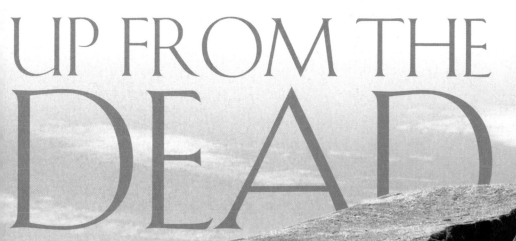

EPILOGUE

The Bible is filled with mysteries, with marvels and wonders that modern science still cannot explain.

This ancient, sacred text invites each of us not to "solve" the mysteries it depicts, but rather to ponder them. The Bible challenges us to explore whether life is more than merely what we can see and feel, measure and quantify.

We are faced with these questions every day. Few of us have not experienced our own moments of mystery, those circumstances that seem to whisper that there is more to life than meets the eye.

The mysteries and stories, parables and events, prophecies and people that make up the Bible were gathered together to lead us on a search for God. And that search is intended to lead us into a relationship with God that will affect us authentically and profoundly.

If we leave the mysteries of the Bible on the page where we've found them, we miss the point. These pages invite us to reach beyond ourselves and our world as we know it, to find a much deeper vision of reality. They invite us to acknowledge the possibility of a God who reaches back. If the Bible teaches us anything, it is that he will.

"Can you understand the mysteries surrounding God All-Powerful? They are higher than the heavens and deeper than the grave. So what can you do when you know so little, and these mysteries outreach the earth and the ocean?"

Job 11:7–9

ACKNOWLEDGMENTS
CREDITS

Rather than a definitive information source, *Inside the Mysteries of the Bible* was written to invite you to explore for yourself how God interacts with his creation, what role faith plays in your journey, and what the life and work of Jesus Christ reveals about God and his relationship with humanity. As we compiled our research, we took great care to question and verify. Now, we offer you the opportunity to research and verify our findings as well.

EDITORIAL SOURCES

The following resources were used to develop the material in this book.
1 Books written on specific topics
2 Bible dictionaries or encyclopedias with entries for each person, place, and significant event
3 Commentaries that explore the Bible text by sections of verses
4 Magazine articles
5 Credible online sources

MAGAZINE ARTICLES

"Do Photos Evidence Lost Edenic River?" by Gordon Govier, October 7, 1996, *Christianity Today*.

"Science and the Miracles of Exodus" by Colin Humphreys, Department of Materials Science & Metallurgy, Cambridge University (full text: europhysicsnews.com/full/33/article6.pdf)

"WHO and Novartis deliver free leprosy treatment for all patients worldwide," *World Health Organization*, accessed 6/12/06 at who.int/mediacentre/news/releases/2005/pr57/en/index.html

BOOKS AND OTHER TEXT PRODUCTS FOR REFERENCE

Breaking the Da Vinci Code, Darrell Bock and Francis Moloney, Nelson Books, 2004

Cracking the Da Vinci Code, Simon Cox, Barnes & Noble, 2004

Holman Bible Dictionary, Trent C. Butler (ed), Broadman & Holman Publishers, 1991

International Standard Bible Encyclopedia, Electronic Edition Parsons Technology, Inc.1998

Miracles or Magic? Andre Kole, Harvest House Publishers, 1987

Secrets of the Code, Dan Burstein (ed), CDS Books, 2004

The Archaeological Study Bible, Zondervan, 2005

The Da Vinci Hoax, Carl Olson, Sandra Miesel, Ignatius Press, 2004

The Learning Bible, American Bible Society, 2000

The New International Dictionary of the Bible, J.D. Douglas & Merrill C. Tenney (ed); Zondervan, 1987

The Truth Behind the Da Vinci Code, Richard Abanes, Harvest House Publishers, 2004

The Zondervan NIV Atlas of the Bible, Zondervan, 1989

Truth and Fiction in the Da Vinci Code, Bart D. Ehrman, Oxford University Press, 2004

Tyndale Bible Dictionary, Walter Elwell, Ph.D., Philip W. Comfort, Ph.D. (ed), Tyndale, 2001

ONLINE SOURCES THAT MAY BE HELPFUL

animal.discovery.com
en.wikipedia.org
evolution-facts.org/Ev-Crunch/c14b.htm
howstuffworks.com
trowandholden.com
usgovinfo.about.com
abu.nb.ca
aish.com
alternet.org
answers.com
bbc.co.uk/science
beyondbelief.com
bibleplaces.com
bibleplus.org
botanical.com
carm.org
catholic.com
cbn.com/entertainment
cesnur.org
chabad.org
christiananswers.net
christianitytoday.com
churchisraelforum.com
crisismagazine.com
crossroadsinitiative.com
ctlibrary.com
danbrown.com

da-vinci-code.nl
eatright.org
europhysicsnews.com
geocities.com
godsquad.com
igs.berkeley.edu
inplainsite.org
jewishencyclopedia.com
jewishgates.com
christiancourier.com
jimgarlow.com
khaleejtimes.com
leaderu.com
louvre.fr
margaretstarbird.net
mindspring.com
muslim-answers.org
mydd.com/story
nashotah.edu
newadvent.org
nps.gov
nytimes.com
olhc.org
opusdei.org
outreach.com/media
partialobserver.com
rockies.net

rosslynchapel.org.uk
sandiegozoo.org
st-edmunds.cam.ac.uk
tektonics.org
theage.com.au
msnbc.msn.com
thedavincichallenge.com
touregypt.net
usc.edu
vrg.org
westminster-abbey.org
who.int/mediacentre
frivolity.com
frivolity.com
geocities.com

ART SOURCES

Art Resource

Leonardo da Vinci (1452-1519)
The Last Supper. Pre-restoration.
Location: S. Maria delle Grazie, Milan, Italy
Photo Credit: Scala / Art Resource, NY

Michelangelo (1475-1564)
Creation of Adam. Detail of the Sistine ceiling.
Locatio: Sistine Chapel, Vatican Palace, Vatican State
Photo Credit: Alinari / Art Resource, NY

Birds entering the ark. Mosaic.
Location: S. Marco, Venice, Italy
Photo Credit: Scala / Art Resource, NY

Brueghel, Pieter the Elder (c.1525-1569)
The Tower of Babel, 1563. Oil on oakwood, 114 x 155 cm.
Location: Kunsthistorisches Museum, Vienna, Austria
Photo Credit: Erich Lessing / Art Resource, NY

Perugino, Pietro (1448-1523)
The Prophets: Isaiah, Moses, Daniel, David, Jeremiah, Solomon.
Lower left of the Lunette with Sibyls and Prophets.
Location: Collegio del Cambio, Palazzo dei Priori (Comunale), Perugia, Italy
Photo Credit: Scala / Art Resource, NY

Fontebasso, Francesco (1709-1769)
Esther and Ahasuerus.
Location: Parish Church, Povo, Italy
Photo Credit: Scala / Art Resource, NY

Liss, Johann (c.1597-1629)
Sacrifice of Isaac.
Location: Uffizi, Florence, Italy
Photo Credit: Scala / Art Resource, NY

Poussin, Nicolas (1594-1665)
The Apotheosis of Saint Paul. Oil on canvas, 128 x 95 cm.
Location: Louvre, Paris, France
Photo Credit: Erich Lessing / Art Resource, NY

Reni, Guido (1575-1642)
The Nativity.
Location: Certosa di S. Martino, Naples, Italy
Photo Credit: Scala / Art Resource, NY

Rubens, Peter Paul (1577-1640)
Incredulity of Saint Thomas, central panel of the Rockox Triptych.
Location: Koninklijk Museum voor Schone Kunsten, Antwerp, Belgium
Photo Credit: Scala / Art Resource, NY

Balaam and His Ass Stopped by an Angel.
Location: Bibliotheque Nationale, Paris, France
Photo Credit: Snark / Art Resource, NY

The Infant Samuel Being Offered to the High Priest Eli. Gothic manuscript. 15th CE.
Location: Bibliotheque Nationale, Paris, France
Photo Credit: Erich Lessing / Art Resource, NY

Persian and Medean Warriors. Relief from the Audience Hall of Darius I (Apadana),
eastern stairway. Achaemenid dynasty, 6th-5th c. BCE.
Location: Persepolis, Iran
Photo Credit: Giraudon / Art Resource, NY

Tissot, James Jacques Joseph (1836-1902) and Followers.
The Ark Passes over Jordan. Gouache on board. 8 3/8 x 10 13/16 in. (21.4 x 27.6cm)
Gift of the heirs of Jacob Schiff, x1952-214. Photo by Joseph Parnell.
Location: The Jewish Museum, New York, NY, U.S.A.
Photo Credit: The Jewish Museum, NY / Art Resource, NY

Gutenberg, Johannes (1390/1400-c.1468)
Biblia Latina. Mainz: Johann Gutenberg & Johann Fust (c.1455).
Volume II, f.131v-132. PML 818 ch1 ff1.
Location: The Pierpont Morgan Library, New York, NY, U.S.A.
Photo Credit: The Pierpont Morgan Library / Art Resource, NY

Scroll of Isaiah. From one of the Dead Sea Scrolls.
Location: Israel Museum (IDAM), Jerusalem, Israel
Photo Credit: Snark / Art Resource, NY

The printing press invented by Johannes Gutenberg between 1397 and 1400.
Location: Gutenberg Museum, Mainz, Germany
Photo Credit: Erich Lessing / Art Resource, NY

Jericho, Israel, The Oasis of Jericho seen against the surrounding desert.
Location: Jericho, Israel
Photo Credit: Erich Lessing / Art Resource, NY

Ein Harod, Israel
Location: Israel
Photo Credit: Erich Lessing / Art Resource, NY

The hills between Beit Shemesh and Jerusalem
Location: Beth-Shemesh, Israel
Photo Credit: Erich Lessing / Art Resource, NY

The Cave of Ein-Gedi
Location: Oasis, En-Gedi
Photo Credit: Erich Lessing / Art Resource, NY

Hippocrates of Kos (often identified with Chrysippos). Marble bust. Height 36 cm. MA 326.
Location : Louvre, Paris, France
Photo Credit: Erich Lessing / Art Resource, NY

Tomb of Lazarus
Location: Bethany, Israel
Photo Credit: Erich Lessing / Art Resource, NY

Dover Electronic Clip Art
Bible Illustrations

FotoSearch
www.fotosearch.com
Christian Faith Vol. 1, Christian Faith Vol. 2, Christian Faith Vol. 3

Getty Images

71057183 (RF) raven
Collection: Stockbyte Silver
Photographer: John Foxx

RL000717 (RF) Michelangelo's *Moses* in Rome, Italy
Collection: Photodisc Green
Photographer: PhotoLink

RL000037 (RF) *Mosaic Deisis Detail*
Collection: Photodisc Green
Photographer: Andrew Ward/Life File

56135346 (RM) *King Louis IX (1217-70) before Damietta,*
illustration from 'Bibliotheque des Croisades' by J-F. Michaud, 1877 (litho)
Collection: The Bridgeman Art Library
Photographer: Gustave Dore

bat173494 (RM) *Solomon Before the Ark of the Covenant,* 1747 (oil on canvas)
Collection: The Bridgeman Art Library
Photographer: Blaise Nicolas Le Sueur

GoodSalt

ImageID: ebsps0262
Moses at Red Sea
Artist: Erik Stenbakken

ImageID: dmtas0125
Elijah and the Ravens
Artist: Darrel Tank

ImageID: lwjas0173
Sodom & Gomorrah
Artist: Lars Justinen

ImageID: pppas0100
King Darius and the Handwriting on the Wall
Artist: Pacific Press Publishing

Hugh Claycombe
Solomon's Temple
Interior cross section
(630) 620-6818, lclaycombe@aol.com

Tapestry Productions
Resurrection Morning
Artist: Ron DiCianni, www.tapestryproductions.com

All other images:
iStock Photo, www.istockphoto.com

History and Mission of the American Bible Society

AMERICAN BIBLE SOCIETY

Since the establishment of the American Bible Society in 1816, its history has been closely intertwined with the history of the nation whose name it bears. In fact, the Society's early leadership reads like a *Who's Who* of patriots and other American movers and shakers. Its first president was Elias Boudinot, formerly the President of the Continental Congress. John Jay, John Quincy Adams, DeWitt Clinton, and chronicler of the new nation James Fenimore Cooper also played significant roles in the Society's history, as would Rutherford B. Hayes and Benjamin Harrison in later generations.

From the beginning, the Bible Society's mission has been to respond to the spiritual needs of a fast-growing, diverse population in a rapidly expanding nation. From the new frontier beyond the Appalachian Mountains, missionaries sent back dire reports of towns that did not have a single copy of the Bible to share among its citizens. State and local Bible Societies did not have the resources, network, or capabilities to fill this growing need: a national organization was called for. The ABS committed itself to organizational and technological innovations to meet the demand. No longer subject to British restrictions, the ABS could set up its own printing plants, develop better qualities of paper and ink, and establish a network of colporteurs to get the Bibles to the people who needed them.

Reaching out to diverse audiences has always been at the heart of ABS's mission. Scriptures were made available to Native peoples in their own languages—in Delaware in 1818, followed soon by Mohawk, Seneca, Ojibwa, Cherokee, and others. French and Spanish Bibles were published for the Louisiana Territory, Florida, and the Southwest. By the 1890s the ABS was printing or distributing Scriptures in German, Portuguese, Chinese, Italian, Russian, Danish, Polish, Hungarian, Czech, and other languages to meet the spiritual needs of an increasing immigrant population. In 1836, 75 years before the first Braille Bibles were produced, the ABS was providing Scriptures to the blind in "raised letter" editions.

Responding to the need for Bibles in the languages and formats that speak most deeply to people's hearts continues to be a priority of the ABS. Through its partnerships with other national Bible Societies, the ABS can provide some portion of Scripture in almost any language that has a written form. It has also been able to provide Braille Scriptures for the blind, as well as recorded Scriptures for the visually impaired, dyslexic, and people who have not yet learned to read.

The Bible Society's founders and their successors have always understood the Bible as a text that can speak to people's deepest needs in times of crisis. During the War of 1812, the ABS distributed its first Scriptures to the military when it provided New Testaments to the crew of the USS *John Adams*. During the Civil War, the ABS provided Testaments to both northern and southern forces, and it has continued to provide Bibles and Testaments to the U.S. military forces during every subsequent war, conflict, and operation. During the painful post-Reconstruction era, when Jim Crow laws prevailed in many parts of the nation, the ABS was able to provide Scriptures to African Americans through its partnership with the Agency Among Colored People of the South and through the historic Black churches.

This faith that the Word of God speaks in special ways during times of crisis continues to inform the ABS mission. In recent years the Bible Society has produced Scripture booklets addressing the needs of people with HIV/AIDS and of those experiencing profound loss due to acts of terrorism and natural disasters.

Translation and scholarship are key components in the Bible Society's mission of communicating the Word of God faithfully and powerfully. In the mid-20th century, the ABS, in partnership with the United Bible Societies, developed innovative theories and practices of translation. First, they insisted that all the Bible translations they sponsored were to be created exclusively by native speakers, with biblical and linguistic experts serving only as translation consultants to provide technical support and guidance. From the lively and heartfelt translations that resulted, Bible Society scholars were able to see the power of translations that were rendered not on a word-for-word basis, but on a meaning-for-meaning basis that respected the natural rhythms and idioms of the target languages. This practice of "functional equivalence" translation reinvigorated the practice of translating the Bible into English and is partly responsible for the explosion of new

translations of the Bible that have been issued in the past thirty years. These include the Bible Society's own *Good News Translation* and *Contemporary English Version*, but also the *New International Version*, *New Revised Standard Version*, *Today's Century Version*, *New Living Translation*, and *The Message*.

As an organization dedicated to preparing well-researched, faithful translations, the ABS has necessarily committed itself to the pursuit of scholarly excellence. In cooperation with the United Bible Societies, the ABS has helped develop and publish authoritative Greek and Hebrew texts, handbooks on the different books of the Bible, dictionaries, and other technical aids. To make sure that all relevant disciplines are explored, the Bible Society's Nida Institute for Biblical Scholarship convenes symposia and conferences that invite both academic specialists and practicing translators to gather and exchange ideas that will assist translators in communicating the Bible's message to new audiences. For churches and readers seeking a deeper understanding of the Bible and its background, the ABS has developed study Bibles, multimedia video translations with DVD extras, Scriptures in special formats, and website resources.

For almost two centuries the American Bible Society has maintained its commitment to innovation and excellence. While the challenges it has faced over the years have changed, the Society's mission has remained constant—*to make the Bible available to every person in a language and format each can understand and afford, so all people may experience its life-changing message.*

To find out more about the American Bible Society please go to www.bibles.com or call 877-THE-BIBLE.

INSIDE THE

OF THE
BIBLE

NEW PERSPECTIVES ON ANCIENT TRUTHS